NFT

All You Need to Know About Investing in Nft

(Application and How to Make Money With Non-fungible Tokens)

Yvonne Landry

Published By **Regina Loviusher**

Yvonne Landry

All Rights Reserved

*Nft: All You Need to Know About Investing in Nft
(Application and How to Make Money With Non-
fungible Tokens)*

ISBN 978-1-77485-727-4

Legal & Disclaimer

The information contained in this ebook is not designed to replace or take the place of any form of medicine or professional medical advice. The information in this ebook has been provided for educational & entertainment purposes only.

The information contained in this book has been compiled from sources deemed reliable, and it is accurate to the best of the Author's knowledge; however, the Author cannot guarantee its accuracy and validity and cannot be held liable for any errors or omissions. Changes are periodically made to this book. You must consult your doctor or get professional medical advice before using any of the suggested remedies, techniques, or information in this book.

Upon using the information contained in this book, you agree to hold harmless the Author from and against any damages, costs, and expenses, including any legal fees potentially resulting from the application of any of the information provided by this guide. This disclaimer applies to any damages or injury caused by the use and application, whether directly or indirectly, of any advice or information presented, whether for breach of contract, tort, negligence, personal injury, criminal intent, or under any other cause of action.

You agree to accept all risks of using the information presented inside this book. You need to consult a professional medical practitioner in order to ensure you are both able and healthy enough to participate in this program.

Table Of Contents

Chapter 1: What Are Nfts? A Brief History Of Nfts, And How You Can Benefit From These

NFTs is an abbreviation for non-fungible tokens. It's a type of digital asset that ensures the the ownership rights of an object or group of items which is stored on blockchains like Ethereum or Solana. Because NFTs can't be duplicated, or altered They are the best choice to track the rights to non-replicable property for instance, images or parcel of land.

For example, a dollar could be exchanged for any other dollar The same is true to cryptocurrency like bitcoin or Ethereum.

However, an NFT On contrary, operates differently. Its value is determined by its scarcity and the proof of its origin, similar to an uncommon postage stamp or a diary. Or an 1952 Topps #311 Mickey Mantle card.

In principle, everything can be created as a non-fungible token (including CryptoPunks' blocks heads and shorter films, domain name names as well as virtual cannabis farm) However, the bulk of the recent interest from investors has been focused on sports and digital art collectibles as well as video games which players can design and control alternate worlds often referred to in the form of "metaverses," or "metaverses").

What are non-fungible tokens?

NFTs are non-fungible. (NFTs) can be described as cryptographically extraordinary tokens that are linked to digital (and sometimes physical) content. They also serve as an evidence of ownership. They are also referred to as digital assets that have the ability to identify information that is stored within smart contracts.

This is the reason why there is a distinct feature of the different NFT and, in turn, they are unable to be replaced in a direct way by a different token. Since each NFTs are the same and therefore, they are not able to be swapped in a similar fashion.

Banknotes are, however they can be swapped one for the other; If they are of similar value, the person who holds them sees no distinction between, say an dollar note and the other.

Bitcoin is a currency that can be used in a variety of ways. It is possible to send one Bitcoin to someoneelse, and they could then send it back towards you. In the end, you'll still possess one Bitcoin. (Of Of course the price of Bitcoin could fluctuate during exchange.) Since fungible tokens are divisible they can be used to transfer or receive lesser amounts than one Bitcoin which is which is measured in the satoshis (think of satoshis in terms of cents of the value of a Bitcoin).

If something is fungible, it is able to be replaced. Oil is fungible since every barrel is unique however, a unique Mickey Mantle rookie card is not a typical baseball card. It's exclusive or not fungible.

When assets that are not fungible are tokenized, the valuable details about the asset is digitalized using the token.

Tokens are kept in wallets with their own unique address. Token IDs are linked to wallet addresses in the blockchain which is a vast open, public database which allows anyone to verify the digital ownership.

This means that counterfeit or counterfeit versions of any NFTs are not accepted as authentic or original.

The tokens that are not fungible are generally not divisible. This is similar to the way you aren't able to send an individual a part or a piece of concert tickets. A part from a ticket to a show will be useless by itself and cannot be exchanged.

Yet certain investors have recently tried out the concept of fractionalized NFTs however, they are in a legal gray zone and may be classified as securities.

The first non-fungible tokens to be released were CryptoKitties collectibles. Every digital kitten that is based on blockchain technology is unique. If you give someone a CryptoKitty, and receive one from a different person the one you receive will be totally different from the one you gave. The purpose for the game's purpose is to gather different digital kittens.

The unique data of a non-fungible currency like the CryptoKitty, is recorded within its contract, and permanently recorded on the Blockchain of the token.

The CryptoKitties initially started out as ERC-721 tokens on Ethereum blockchain However, they have since moved to their own blockchain, Flow, to make them more accessible to cryptocurrency novices.

A Brief History of NFTS

Who came up with NFTs A Story About The Man Who Invent the first NFT

Where did this trend in technology come from? The 3rd of May 2014, the history of NFTs and the person who came up with their creation, Kevin McCoy, began. McCoy coined his non-fungible token "Quantum" well before the cryptocurrency art market started to grow.

What is the story with Quantum?

Kevin McCoy's Quantum is a pixelated picture of an octagon that is filled with arcs, circles or other shapes sharing the same central area, with larger forms that surround smaller ones, and then hypnotically flashing in bright colors. This unique "Quantum" artwork (2014-2021) is currently on auction at $7 million.

McCoy is an outstanding. His wife and husband Jennifer have established a name for themselves as top digital artists over the course of time. This NFT concept is rooted in the world of art. it was born out of an extensive history of artists exploring the possibilities of technologies.

Their work has often been bought by enthusiastic collectors of art However, McCoy would rather sell their work at an exhibition or one-on- one, rather than participate taking part in bidding wars in public auctions. Their piece "Every Shot Each Episode" has been displayed at The Metropolitan Museum of Art.

What is the NFTS System?

Tokens like Bitcoin or ERC-20 tokens that are based on Ethereum are not fungible. ERC-721 is Ethereum's token that is non-fungible. standard, used by platforms like CryptoKitties as well as Decentraland.

Non-fungible tokens can also be created using non-fungible token tools and support on other smart-contract-enabled blockchains.

While Ethereum is the first blockchain to experience broad adoption of the blockchain ecosystem is growing, with blockchains like Solana, NEO, Tezos, EOS, Flow, Secret Network, and TRON support NFTs.

Smart contracts allow the inclusion of more specific characteristics like the owner's name rich metadata, secure files.

The ability of tokens that are not fungible to permanently prove ownership of digital assets is a major step in a world that is becoming increasingly digital.

It is possible to imagine blockchain's promises of secure and trustless security applying to the exchange or ownership of almost every asset.

Protocols for tokens that are non-fungible and smart contract technology is still being developed, just as it is the case with blockchain up to now. However, the development of platforms and applications that are decentralized to manage and develop of non-fungible tokens is an issue.

There's also the problem of creating an industry standard. Blockchain development is a bit dispersed, with numerous individuals working on own projects. To succeed, unification of protocols and interoperability might be needed.

What is it that makes NFTS so special? What can they be used for?

Non-fungible tokens are unique in their features and are usually tied to an asset. They are used to prove ownership of digital objects like game skins to physical assets.

Other tokens, such as notes and coins can be fungible. And when they are exchanged they have the same characteristics and worth. They are the same

Non-fungible tokens are a great way to represent digital collectibles , such for

CryptoKitties, NBA Top Shot and Sorare in addition to digital assets that must be distinguished from each other to show their worth or their scarcity.

They may serve as a symbol for anything, from virtual parcels of land to artworks to ownership certificates. They are also traded and bought through NFT exchanges.

While dedicated marketplaces such OpenSea and Rarible were previously the dominant players in the market however, some of the most reputable cryptocurrency exchanges have recently started to get involved.

Binance announced the NFT marketplace on June 20, 2021. Coinbase announced plans to launch their private NFT marketplace in the month of October 2021. The marketplace saw more than 1.4 million customers who signed up to the waitlist within the first 48 hours.

Who is the person who can create NFTS?

A NFT can be made by anyone from entrepreneurs to artists, corporations, art enthusiasts filmmakers, authors, social media stars as well as regular people like us. There is no prerequisite for experience or experience is required, and anyone can create an NFT in the event that they are able to prove that they wrote or legally owned the content.

Chapter 2: What Are Erc-721 Tokens?

Since the interface was initially made available in the form of the EIP in September of 2017, ERC721 tokens, also called NFTs, also known as Non-Fungible Tokens (NFTs) are a topic that has been the focus of developers' interest. They allow developers to represent ownership for any kind of information, thus broadening the range of data that can be used as tokens in Ethereum. Ethereum blockchain.

Non-fungible tokens stand out by the fact that each is tied to a unique identifier giving each token a unique identity to the owner of it. This is quite different from tokens built upon the ERC20 token standard, a token that is fungible, meaning every token can be interchangeable. Developers are able to create any token within a single contract based on an ERC20 standard token. But, each token within the standard ERC721 token is assigned an individual meaning.

ERC721 is an unfungible standard token interface This implies that ERC721 tokens are just one of the subsets of Ethereum tokens.

Understanding the ERC721 Standards

The ERC721 standard, as with other token standards before it, defines the general guidelines that all tokens on the Ethereum network must follow to attain the expected outcomes. Token standards typically define the following attributes of an individual token:

How do you determine ownership?

What is the process of creating tokens?

What is the process of transferring tokens?

How do tokens get burned?

ERC721 is vital for a variety of reasons, not least the numerous uses it allows and its ability to integrate seamlessly into the ecosystem infrastructure. Non-fungible tokens are more important due to the fact that they have a an established interface that wallet and exchange operators are able to easily apply. Integration into the ecosystem makes non-fungible assets more liquid and helps in price discovery and lets everyone own the same tokens anywhere around the globe.

ERC721 Games Using ERC721

Non-fungible tokens have led to new kinds of digital objects that are collectible as well as a brand new blockchain-based game infrastructure. Many developers have mixed the two and one of them, CryptoKitties, has become an instant success.

CryptoKitties has developed the collectibles usage case, and proved that people are interested in things that are digitally scarce. The owners should be confident that their property will are not duplicated or taken due to the fact that

CryptoKitties utilizes an ERC721 standard token as well as it is part of the Ethereum network. The token standard ERC721 has been utilized by many games to create their platforms. Decentraland tokenizes every parcel of virtual land in order to create unique tokens, which allow players to purchase rare, virtual real estate in the universe. The tokens that are non-fungible can open up huge amounts of gaming assets' liquidity and allow gamers to enjoy distinct experiences.

What exactly is ERC1155?

The Ethereum Network ERC-1155 is a token standard developed by Enjin which is able to create functional (currencies) as well as non-fungible (digital pets, cards, and game skins) properties. ERC-1155 tokens are secure as well as tradable and secure because of their connection to the Ethereum network.

Visit EIP 1155 to find out more about the ERC-1155 standards.

ERC-1155 is an innovative method for creating tokens that permit more efficient trades and transaction bundling, leading to savings in costs. The standard for tokens allows utilitarian tokens (like $BNB and $BAT) as well as other non-fungible ones (like CryptoKitties) to be developed.

ERC-1155 has optimizations that allow transactions to be safer and efficient. The cost of trading tokens can be cut down when transactions are bundled. ERC-1155 was developed from prior work like ERC-20 (utility tokens) and ERC-721 (security tokens) (rare unique collectibles that are only available for a short time).

What are the crypto kitties?

The players can adopt, train and trade virtual cats in Cryptokitties which is a virtual game. Axiom Zen, a blockchain company with its headquarters in Vancouver developed the game. But, the most important thing to remember is that this is the first time that DAPP has been utilized to play games for recreation and leisure.

Cryptokitties are selling out of the shelves. The crypto kits are being sold at a price of more than one million dollars. There have been reports of people earning more by trading in cryptocurrencies than investing the money in an IRA!

Background

CryptoKitties are a non-fungible currency (NFT) that is unique in each CryptoKitty and operates on Ethereum's main blockchain network. Each CryptoKitty is unique and is owned by the user and is backed through the Blockchain. Its value fluctuates in line with the market. Even game developers can't replicate or move CryptoKitties with the consent of the user. Users can interact through their CryptoKitties by purchasing, selling or siring (breeding) them. The CryptoKitty artwork on the other hand is not part of the blockchain but is owned through Axiom Zen. The artwork was made available under a new "Nifty" license that allows users to use the CryptoKitty's image in limited ways.

On the 19th of October on the 19th of October, 2017 at ETH Waterloo, an Ethereum hackathon, a trial version of CryptoKitties was launched. Genesis was the first as well as the most costly pet was auctioned off to the public for ETH246.9255 (US$117,712) in December 2nd, 2017.

Virtual cats can be crossed, and each is unique and has a an 256-bit genome that contains traits and DNA that can be passed down to the offspring. Certain traits are passed on between parents and their kids. Shape, pattern eye shape, hair, background color highlights color and eye color the possibility of wildness, setting "prestige," and even secret are just a few of the attributes that can be found in every cat. Other traits, like cooling down time are characteristics of the offspring's "generation," that is greater than the highest generation of the parents.

CryptoKitties was split into its own company, Dapper Labs, on the 20th of March, 2018, and has raised 12 million from leading venture capitalists as well as angel investors. Union Square Ventures in New York and Andreessen Horowitz in San Francisco was the lead investors in the round.

A CryptoKitty was auctioned off for $140,000 on May 12, 2018. Stephen Curry, an American professional basketball player was the first celebrity-branded CryptoKitty that was unveiled in the name of CryptoKitties in May of this year. Curry received three CryptoKitties that featured exclusive images to be part of the package, the first one Curry auctioned off. It was then stopped by the company, who claimed it was because Stephen Curry was not as in the market as they thought. Concerning all the Stephen Curry collectibles, the firm was later sued for theft of trade secrets. The court ruled in the favor of the business, saying, "The evidence shows that Defendant and not Plaintiff was the one who came up with the idea of granting digital collectors a license with the likenesses of celebrities first. ..."

With 3.2 million transactions through their smart contracts CryptoKitties crossed the million cats mark in October. Dapper Labs, which developed CryptoKitties after it was spun off of Axiom Zen was able to raise an additional $15 million from Venrock's venture round in November. The company's value increased by a third.

The German museum ZKM Center for Art and Media Karlsruhe utilized

CryptoKitties to show blockchain technology in the year 2018.

What is crypto punk?

CryptoPunks was released for the first time in June 2017 and was developed by a team of two at American Game Studio Larva Labs comprising Matt Hall and John Watkinson. They've developed algorithms to create 24x24-pixel art-based images. CryptoPunks were first released then and then CryptoKitties. They're leaders in the NFT market and were a catalyst in the development of ERC-721 tokens. These tokens are, unlike ERC-20 tokens are unique in their own way.

In the Ethereum (ETH) Blockchain there is a collection of 10,000 CryptoPunk characters, each with the proof of ownership. Most of the 10,000 characters are human However, there are 88 Zombies and 24 Apes and 9 Aliens have been identified as distinctive punks.

CryptoPunk 7804 One of the nine alien NFTs was purchased to a buyer for ETH4200 (roughly $7.5 million) on March 10. It was probably the most costly NFT ever sold in a single day, however Beeple's Everyday: The First 5000 Days, which sold at Christie's for $69 million the following day, was a lot more expensive. Ethereum account 0xf4b4a58974524e183c275f3c6ea895bc2368e738 purchased Punk 7804. This is the first transaction of the account using the Ethereum blockchain of any kind.

0x03911fecabd6b4809c88e2e6eb856ec932b2ee3e, the account that sold the Punk, first purchased it on January 10th, 2018 for 12ETH (worth USD15,000 at the time). After its initial investment the account has earned huge profits. On the 21st February 2021, it also bought the account to Ape CryptoPunk for 800ETH (USD1.2 million).

Top NFT Project

1. FLOW

It is the Flow NFT token was intended to be the platform for a brand new type of gaming, apps as well as digital assets and also a fast and easy to develop blockchain. It is a blockchain that is layer-one developed by a team of developers that has extensive experience with consumer blockchain applicationslike CryptoKitties, Dapper Wallet, and of course, NBA Top Shot. NBA Top Shot.

FLOW can be bought on cryptocurrency exchanges like Kraken or Gate.

2. ENJIN

Enjin is a company that has an interconnected ecosystem of digital goods that make trading and monetizing gaming-related products easy for all. It lets game developers tokenize their game-related objects on Ethereum and is backed with Enjin Coin that is an ERC 20 token developed by Enjin. It has a market value of more than one billion dollars, which makes it the most important NFT in March 3 2021. Enjin coin is among the cheapest coins that has a huge potential for growth in 2021, based on our analysis.

Enjin Coin is available for purchase through cryptocurrency exchanges, such as Binance, Bithumb, Uniswap, Balancer, and others.

3. MANA

Decentraland (MANA) Decentraland (MANA) is an immersive Virtual Reality (VR) platform that is based on Ethereum that lets users "create research, create, and make money from applications and content." The users can purchase lots of land in order to use, build and sell according to their own preferences. As of January 20, 2021 Aetheria is a Cyberpunk themed district that has a total of 8,008 LANDs is the biggest district (each LAND area is approximately 100 square Metres). Anyone else getting Ready Player One vibes? The project was launched with a profit of $24 million initial coin offer (ICO) which was followed by the virtual world scheduled to be open by February 2020.

The ERC-20 (MANA) and one ERC-721 (LAND) token is used in Decentraland. MANA is to be burnt to generate Land tokens, each which equals 100 square meters of land in the metaverse (virtual real land).

MANA Coin is available for purchase at cryptocurrency exchanges which include Binance, OKEx, and Coinbase Pro.

4. Axie Infinity

Axie Infinity is cryptocurrency-based fighting and trading game that is partly controlled and operated by players. It is a Pokemon-inspired Axie Infinity, a game which lets players gather breed, fight, and exchange tokenized battle animals also known as Axies.

These Axies are available in many dimensions and shapes. There are over 500 body parts available to pick from, each one with its own uniqueness as well as drop rates. Axies may be genetically modified in order to create larger Axies (up to seven) and then be offered for sale through Axie market. Axie market. Axie Infinity is a participant in the governance vote with Axie Infinity, the Axie Infinite Shards (AXS) the token of ERC-20.

Binance is the sole place where you can purchase AXS.

5. Terra Virtua Kolect

Terra Virtua Kolect is an NFT crypto market that provides NFT collectors and developers with an organized multi-platform (PC Mobile, AR/VR, PC) ecosystem. TVK has raised $2.6 million through token sales to major digital media firms like Legendary Entertainment and Paramount Pictures. The digital asset is accessible online, through the mobile application, and also in 3D with Augmented Reality in this NFT cryptocurrency project.

TVK can be purchased through cryptocurrency exchanges such as Binance, Uniswap, Bitmax 1inch, and many more.

6. Origin Protocol

Origin Protocol, also known as DShop in the NFT cryptocurrency community is a decentralized online shopping network. The DShop allows purchasing NFTs as demonstrated by 3LAU's latest NFT drop, where 33 distinct NFTs were auctioned off for $11,684,101 the 26th of February 2021. The auction was held for the first time that a musical note was tokenized in a collection, and "is just the beginning for musicians to grasp the huge value they bring to every corner of the planet," according to 3LAU.

OGN is available for purchase via cryptocurrency exchanges, such as Binance, Huobi, Uniswap and many more.

7. Chromia

Chromia Studios, a blockchain platform that allows users to develop dApps was launched in August of 2019 in collaboration together with Workinman Interactive. Chromia is planning to fund the development of MMOGs (Massively Multiplayer Online Games) that are entirely run on blockchain technology, as well as NFTs. Mines of Dalarmia is their initial release is a game that mines featuring economics and ownership features which can be played on different platforms.

CHR is available for purchase via cryptocurrency exchanges like Binance, Huobi Global, Upbit, Bithumb, Binance JEX.

8. Rare

Rarible offers an NFT marketplace that is centered on creators and utilizes RARI, the original RARI token. Anyone can build NFT crypto to create unique digital goods. The NFT cryptocurrency marketplace is fully operational. To help the platform grow the platform uses a part of the profits to fund the initial mint transaction which is where the NFT is created. The RARI token is limited to a maximum of 25,000,000 and an Rarible NFT marketplace receiving the vast majority of tokens.

RARI can be purchased through cryptocurrency exchanges such as Uniswap, Mooniswap, Balancer and more.

9. WAX

The Worldwide Asset Exchange (WAX) is known as"the "King of NFTs"" is soon to partner with CAPCOM to provide ERC-721 and ERC-1155 tokens (Multi-tokens which support fungible as well as non-fungible types of tokens). WAX has been utilized by well-known brands, such as Deadmau5, Atari, William Shatner, Capcom, and Topps to start their NFT cryptocurrency sales.

WAXP is available for purchase via cryptocurrency exchanges like Huobi

Global, Upbit, Bithumb, HitBTC, KuCoin and many more.

10. The Sandbox

The Sandbox is a second blockchain-based platform which allows developers to make money from a specific digital asset type through the blockchain, which is known by the name of VOXEL properties. The Sandbox along with its NFT marketplace, permits users to create VOXEL games and assets using VoxEdit and Game Maker tools. VoxEdit along with the Game Maker tools. The transactions are conducted using an utility token SAND and there will never be 3 billion of them.

SAND is available for purchase through cryptocurrency exchanges, such as Binance, Huobi Global, CoinTiger, Upbit, and other exchanges.

Chapter 3: More Information On The Capabilities And Uses Of Nfts

This book has already discussed several ways the way that NFTs are used in real-world applications However we've only touched the very top of the mountain regarding its capabilities and usage. In the realms in Art, Music, and Gaming specifically We are set to see a significant change in how business is conducted. In this chapter, we're going to examine the key sectors of NFT potential and how they could impact our lives.

Capabilities of NFT for Art

Non-Fungible Tokens allow artworks to be able to be protected by digital signatures that are attached to them, meaning regardless of the number of copies an artwork could be produced the original tokenized version remains as an individual fixture on the Blockchain. Therefore, the artist can still manage the original work and keep any profits generated from it. Perhaps more importantly they eliminate the traditional middleman in the sense that they deal with galleries, art agencies, and promoters.

All one needs to do is make the tokenized NFT representation of their work on blockchain, and it will be available for everyone to view. It's an extremely broad definition of what could be called art in the first instance. It doesn't matter if it's a full-color painting or an adorable meme, it could be placed on the blockchain using its unique Non-Fungible Token that will symbolize it. There's no requirement for an intermediary or critic to participate in the procedure.

NFTs are also a way to ensure that the artist receive a share of the profits every time an NFT is bought. Due to the accountability of the blockchain, any royalties will be properly transferred to the correct recipient. This is a game changer since artworks can be easily copied by online users. In the future, regardless of the number of copies an artwork are created however, the NFT original that is locked in the data block in the blockchain system will be a true original. Thus, the owner of the work is entitled to the benefits that this distinction gives.

And if you're the purchaser of this artwork, NFTs could also be beneficial. Like someone who invested in a prized physical painting years ago, anyone who is willing to spend money on an impressive digital work of art will get rewarded when the art piece improves in value and increases value as time passes. In this way purchasing an NFT supported piece of art isn't just an acquisition of material, it is also a long-term investment for the purchaser.

Capabilities of NFT for Games

In case you didn't know that the gaming industry online is massive and is only expected to grow bigger as time passes by. The games give players lots of flexibility, however, at the end of the day, they're managed by the central control of the businesses that make and maintain these games. If, for instance, you had required to pay for a cost to make use of certain assets/goodies/perks within the game, you are not fully owned.

Since you are only able to play within the rules of the designer. When you have quit the game that item is gone. NFTs are, however may not just allow the ownership of an item for a lifetime, but let a player get an object taken from one of the games and apply it in a different. The items that are leveled-up from games can even become collectibles that are offered in other games, increasing their worth significantly.

As you might have guessed the buying selling, trading, and buying of goods collected will likely turn into an actual game. The possibilities of NFT when it comes to it's role in shaping gaming are quite impressive. At the time of moment, we're in the early stages of what Non-Fungible Tokens could mean. Due to the possibilities and potential of NFT it is likely that there will be more surprises for players further into the future.

Ability of NFT to play music

In many ways the internet has proved to be an opportunity and disadvantage for musicians and the entire music industry. For new musicians looking to establish an impression and make a name for themselves, the possibility to eliminate the middleman and publish videos of themselves performing songs directly on YouTube is sure to make the process of gaining recognition simpler. However, for already established musicians The fact that their music will be posted on the internet , where it can be duplicated and shared for free and certainly makes an enormous dent in their sales records.

There was a time when an artist recording could earn some income from royalties earned from sales of their records however, after the free access internet for everyone became popular, they could not earn as much. The main source of income for many famous artists today is concerts, rather than recordings. However, this source of income took a serious loss during the pandemic in the first half of 2020, making some musicians unable to make ends meet from the earnings generated from streaming services.

The advent of NFT However, it could begin to change the way that the music industry conducts business again. By securing the blockchain, musicians can be sure to receive their royalties from their music. They also benefit since they don't have to pay fees that are that are associated with other methods of buying music digitally. The purchaser can also turn into an investor and the NFT may become a sort of collector's item , which will increase in value with time.

Who can own and buy NFTs?

With all the fantastic topics we've covered regarding the potential of NFTs However, there are those of you are wondering who is able to own and purchase NFTs? The answer is simple , folks--just about everyone and anyone is able to! If you spot a stunning piece of music, artwork or a component of the game you'd like to buy, and have an online wallet and the right cryptocurrency in hand you can become one of the owners or more of the digital items.

You can own a significant work of art, courtesy of Beeple or Beeple or even Beeple, and it could be similar to having the work of Rembrandt and Picasso.

Music recordings can become collectibles, and when you play the right cards it could grow in value, too. Gaming aspects are becoming major investments in the world of virtual as people queue up to purchase vast areas in digital space. The future is a lot of possibilities in terms of those who are able to purchase NFTs, so you are free to join the bandwagon!

Chapter 4: The Economics Of Nft

take advantage of the increasing popularity of cryptocurrency while remaining secure and safe investors must invest in a token that has a value added service and business strategy. Coin projects that are based on cutting-edge technological advancements are currently dominating with new offerings, and it's hard for anyone who is new to figure out whether an ICO is a feasible business plan.

According to us, NFT tokens are more likely to be successful over other tokens as they offer a unique value-added service.

As an ecosystem hub for the cryptocurrency sector which is built on technology. Investors can also benefit from a vast community of high-net-worth individuals within the cryptocurrency sector including the ability to train, educate, mentor cross-promotion and other.

In the end investors can use NFT tokens as an asset and currency as well as a asset or token within the blockchain ecosystem because the tokens aren't custodial and are encrypted right from the beginning.

The ability to access NFT tokens for novice as well as experienced investors. To purchase NFT tokens, utilize fiat currencies such as dollars euro, yen or euros, and trade them in for bitcoins by using Kraken.

In comparison to other currencies, that require both the fiat currency and BTC or both fiat and alt-coins this gives new investors an edge.

Exchanges that are not part of the platform are accessible for trading tokens. Tokens that are traded on other exchanges can be converted into the fiat currency in two easy steps.

Once we recognize an opportunity for market development we are captivated by its potential and possibility of its the success.

A large crowd of users, investors as well as developers will profit from NFT's capability to provide an exchange platform for Bitcoin exchanges to showcase new cryptocurrency and increase their liquidity as well as to launch new value-added services.

NFT is currently the 6th most traded cryptocurrency around the globe and is being the 9th-most traded currency in the realm of blockchain, due to its rapid growth.

Up to the present, NFT token is the sole utility token on the cryptocurrency market with a an operational product.

The first utility token on the bitcoin market to be an operational product. Because it's built using a decentralized system it has the stated goal of making use of the blockchain to significantly influence the world.

It is a goal that has been stated of using blockchain technology to transform the world. are many applications that can be developed based on NFT.

NFT buying and selling NFT

It's too early to know if it's ICO was an success or not. This project was in the works for several years and is led by an experienced staff, and has been supported by a group of investors who are authorized to invest.

A market value of $500 million represents the equivalent of less than 0.5 percent of the total number of Bitcoins currently in circulation. A ICO such as this is the first major evaluation of a new token's popularity and its possible application in the present ecosystem.

Despite its many applications, Bitcoin has remained a utility token due to its small market capitalization.

Partly, this is because the value of utility tokens is directly proportional to their value.

A company that has an estimated valuation in the range of $91.4 billion, similar to PayPal, Inc. (NASDAQ:PYPL) is a company with an average share price of the company's annual cumulative sales of 12 months.

The price of the share of PayPal is 2.2 per cent of value of all global commerce transactions made online in the last year in the event that PayPal is the primary payment processor for E-commerce.

Because the use of the service and its usage are limited and limited, the value of the token is directly related with its amount of transactions.

NFT is expected to take a similar route in the hope of becoming a common currency on exchanges within the next few years too. In other words it will function as the payment tokens currently utilized in the Bitcoin market. This implies that the worth that the currency will increase when more exchanges are willing to accept it.

It is also anticipated that the cost of tokens will increase because more people will purchase as well as sell the tokens.

The first, NFT will be the first utility token that is developed.

It is very likely that NFT will reach its goal to become the standard token in the exchange of digital currencies due to the early stage and the massive amount of backing that it's received from members of the Bitcoin community.

We've seen previously utility tokens such as BTC, Ethereum, and Litecoin in addition to Bitcoin Cash, Dogecoin, and Ripple in the realm of cryptocurrency.

Similar to how I am interested in the potential for the technology, I'm also also interested in the possibilities of a standard. In the cryptocurrency market,

BTC can assist us to get things moving and enable the ecosystem to operate in tandem. However, we require an infrastructure to support it, and Ethereum as well as the Tangle can provide us with this. I hope to see that in the near future, no matter what asset it is representing the tokens will all be called NFTs. As a token owner I get my daily dose of each of BTC and ETH in addition to the other ones. My preferred token could be traded for the one that is the most well-known. My top tokens will be on the market for a bit longer, but without having to invest a an inordinate amount of time studying and mastering the latest NFT this is an excellent thing.

Since NFT as well as other cryptocurrencies share the same value idea, it is broadly accepted by bitcoin community.

I have previously written Seeking Alpha pieces about utility tokens, including "The coming tidal wave of utility tokens" and "Ethereum A Unique and innovative utility Token," to get an idea of what I think about the topic.

There are numerous benefits and uses for utility tokens that I'll write about in my article, such as the following:

* There are no transaction fees, or the threat of transaction cost are in place;

Payment confirmations will be rewarded by an incentive for payment

* Incentive programs for buyers and miners;

* Clearly voting for or against any particular decision creating a sense unity.

* Keeping a defined inventory of consumer goods markets

The quality of the product can be judged by the customers and merchants may establish their own platform to sell their products or services.

My opinion is that utility tokens have a huge impact on the cryptocurrency exchange market. The importance and utility of utility tokens has never been more evident than now that the earlier scaling issues that were associated with crypto-currency charges for exchange have now been addressed.

The cost of NFT will increase with the increase in people who be using it to replace BTC, ETH, etc. when a significant portion of exchanges adopt NFT.

A lot of small, medium and large companies (SMBs) and even larger corporations that have annual sales of the hundreds or tens of millions will recognize the value of NFT in the coming years and will recognize the value of this token.

Blockchain technology and cryptocurrency have always had figures, but it's only that they are now maturing to the point that blockchain companies are able to design their visions of their future, with all the flexibility and freedom they need.

Due to its extensive documentation, including its original Satoshi White Paper on the subject, and a rapidly expanding community, and a huge amount of enthusiasm in support of NFT, Blockchain.info is a great place to start working on and understanding NFT.

To use and participate in NFT Asset Exchange's exchange services and various financial products, you do not require the NFT token.

If you're an active participant in Nxt, or the Nxt community, you'll receive tokens for free by signing up to the Nxt mailing list. NFT tokens are easy to trade with Nxt's Asset Exchange if you hold the tokens on a third-party exchange.

NFT transaction fundamentals

When you pay an "token subscription" anyone who pays receives a token supply which could be exchanged for other items. The subscription can be used to exchange and/or spend without restrictions.

The freebie bundle is a pre-configured bundle to allow trading on the exchange which comes with a variety of tokens which can be traded. In the freebie bundle, you can't select which tokens you wish to purchase Instead, you receive random tokens of tokens from Nxt Asset Exchange. Nxt Asset Exchange, including the various types of tokens (bundles). The other type of freebie bundle is a completely custom-designed package that can be customized to meet your specific needs.

You can exchange any tokens included in the bundle, and also tokens with completely bespoke characteristics. In comparison to other options the freebie pack is less extensive in terms of traded tokens.

There is no need to send an exchange URL for the free package if you purchased the bundle in cash.

What are the possibilities for you to look forward to when you deposit NFT tokens?

The near-term future tokens will soon be traded. They will begin to appear within your account the moment you start to use the wallet.

How many tokens can be traded? What's the max amount of tokens which can be traded on a single exchange?

An account that has a substantial account or with a substantial balance is required to swap over 1000 coins per transaction with NFT.

When is a transaction completed?

The time limit for exchange transactions is visible in your account when you transfer funds to the exchange. But, you can view the balance of your account, go to the page for trades and look up transaction information.

The NFT platform, what do the user add additional tokens?

NFT tokens can be added to accounts in a straightforward manner. To obtain free tokens you do not need to create an account with a brand new user or sign up for an account.

To connect the newly created account with NFT, to link the new account with NFT network, utilize your existing wallet for transfer of tokens you bought with the "freebie package" onto the account. These tokens can now be used for trading and use.

This doesn't require the creation of a new account or registration. Instead you can add tokens that you've bought over the last couple of months onto your current account.

What happens if the exchange is not working?

Contrary to other blockchain networks Nxt Blockchain players have access to additional features not accessible to the public.

A seller of tokens can be directly contacted to discover the reason for the issue If the seller does not respond within 24 hours you may complain to the supervisor.

There is a possibility for a supervisor to temporarily defer or delay the deadline of a transaction when it's recorded, which allows sellers and buyers a bit of flexibility.

Are you concerned about the transaction? how can I handle this instance?

Tokens purchased from the free package can be added to an current account or you may create a new account for the tokens you've bought in the last couple of months and transfer them to the new address.

You are able to utilize your newly created address to obtain tokens from the free package. In this way, you will not be left with a stale exchange account.

What can cause a transaction go wrong?

If the funds aren't in line or if you are able to meet a limit on the quantity of a particular item that you can buy with the money you've provided in the transaction, it will be rejected and you'll have be patient for the supervisor to deny or extend the deadline to complete the transaction.

Do you have any issues on the page that reviews protocol?

The page for reviewing protocols will usually be reviewed within a couple of hours after receiving an inquiry by the user community. A rate of 20% error is a sign that if you are waiting more than that time it is recommended to contact the exchange operator to find out whether they can assist you.

What's wrong with me? Protocol review page?

There are many people who need to make errors to make sure that it functions properly. The "very terrible" mistakes aren't displayed because they're not legible. They can be closed using a checkbox click.

What time will the review take to show up at my door?

Just a few minutes are all it takes to analyze the exchange transaction. Progress bars are typically displayed by the operator after an audit has been completed to show what the exchange transaction has been going.

You can visit the review page for protocol to find out the progress of your transaction once it is filed.

What can I do to return my money if the transaction is not accepted?

The program will show a progress bar showing the current status of the transaction in case the exchange is not successful.

You can ask that the transaction to be approved by establishing an entirely new transaction.

The operator will look into the answer to the first step. The operator will add the transaction to the authorized transactions list in the event that it proves to be positive.

For the first 100 blocks it will then be marked as rejected if it does not receive acceptance. In the event of rejection, it will be deleted off the Exchange's databases.

If I forget these coins, how happens? take place?

Check out these terms and conditions prior to enrolling on an exchange. After the money is transferred from your account into the trading platform, they're not yours anymore.

If you sign in to the exchange program and then click "admin," the same situation occurs. The coins belong to the exchange and not yours to keep.

Don't put off a decision If you're having problems. Contact your bank. Within 48 hours of not receiving a response, you should contact the relevant authorities. You can get your cash back.

How can I trade NFT?

There aren't any restrictions on banks because it's an alternative to traditional currency (such like the US dollar). Any exchange, including but not restricted to exchanges that deal in bitcoin, ethereum, and dash, you can trade your NFTs. In the moment you are able to trade NFT in exchange for bitcoin, dash and Ethereum on these exchanges.

Trading NFT using an exchange like Coinbase as well as Kraken is the best alternative and you must receive your money in the earliest possible time prior to the influx in new clients.

Which are the regulations regarding NFT trading?

A custom Ethereum client known as Devy lets users buy and sell NFT in anonymity under the existing Coin Control regulatory system that is in operation. This means that there is no KYC process in the case of NFT purchase or sale.

Anyone who has purchased NFT could later decide to sell NFT through the Ethereum market to earn an income. If you want to sell your NFT it is necessary to trade them in exchanges or locate a buyer on the blockchain. There is no guarantee that an exchange will take your NFT.

There's no government or organization that is responsible for regulating or approving cryptocurrency transactions. Bitcoin dealers could be a viable option in case you aren't sure of the laws of your state regarding NFTs. To purchase NFT using this method it is necessary to make a cryptocurrency-based payment and not purchase any other coins in the process.

Are NFT transactions possible via blockchain?

Apart from Dash, which is the Dash blockchain, it's not practical to move NFT out of Dash due to the NFT's non-centralized nature. The company behind NFT believes this will be changed in the near future.

Are my coins of any financial value?

To be honest, it's an acceptable thing to ask. The worth of Bitcoin has increased gradually throughout time. It's difficult to answer the answer if not familiar with the concept of digital currency and the science behind cryptography. The value of NFT is completely random and is based on the need for it.

NFT's value NFT is likely to increase when it appears to be more in demand. The value decreases when the demand is less that the available.

What are the negative effects of this?

In order to understand the volatility NFTs can be, it is essential to understand that the value of NFT is determined solely by the financial metrics that are arbitrary.

What could go wrong?

There isn't a central bank because NFT is not centralized. Individuals may not be able buy NFTs in the event that their value drops to a low level.

Are these investments a wise one for my business?

It's a complex question, but the solution is that it depends on a myriad of variables. In the absence of any guidelines that govern the situation, it could be a very risky and possibly profitable investment strategy.

The price of Dash as which is a bitcoin-like alternative, risen dramatically over the last year. There appears to be an increasing demand for Dash as an alternative to bitcoin. to bitcoin, and it is now under scrutiny since its value has continued to climb.

Investors must be aware of their $1.4 billion value of the market and the backing by the highest level of federal government. While the future of NFT remains unclear it is expected to increase significantly over the next few months.

Don't sell your items through eBay or Etsy If you plan to be involved into the cryptocurrency market or NFT market. If you buy something from an online cryptocurrency store you'll have to pay a deposit before you access the product.

To protect customers from scams, NFT should be controlled in this way. The way it is promoted. There is a chance that the platform used to buy NFT might not exist anymore because it's a brand new product. If that doesn't happen new buyers will be introduced to the market to buy NFTs which means the value of the NFTs they've purchased may decline.

It's your choice whether or not you'll accept NFT as a method of payment.

NFT is available to purchase as a gift , if you do not intend to sell it. This makes it unnecessary to keep it in your online storage.

Chapter 5: Crypto & Ethereum

In the past there was a general belief that online dating was only for people who were losers. Nowadays, it's extremely common and accepted in the social sphere. The conventional wisdom is usually incorrect, and those who dismiss the latest trends are those who are missing out on the benefits of these movements. A decade ago, Bitcoin proved to be a daring and enjoyable small experiment in the field of technical libertarianism. Nowadays, large corporations, banks as well as governments and hedge funds have taken cryptocurrency extremely and seriously.

We've been told that there will be an explosion of the cryptocurrency market and a scenario in which everybody loses all their wealth. It's been a long time, but there's no indication that of this happening. Financial experts are making use of cryptocurrency as a hedge against the effects of inflation and fluctuations in currency value. The cost of cryptocurrency fluctuates between a low and a high, sometimes extremely quickly however, over the long-term the trend is always upward.

To fully comprehend NFTs First, we need to know about the cryptocurrency market, and specifically Ethereum (ETH).

What is cryptocurrency?

If you ask someone who is a computer expert on the subject, they may make it seem more complex than it actually is. It's a simple concept and anyone can comprehend the concept without any technical terms.

Cryptocurrency isn't technically considered to be a currency. Courts have decided on this matter and concluded that it's an electronic asset and not an actual currency. There are some important distinctions between these two entities legally, but we'll leave that discussion for an additional chapter. It's a storage device of value and also a means of exchange, much like gold was once.

In today's economy, the majority of money is on paper, not paper. The majority of money is stored on banks' computers than is actually physical paper-based cash. The reason the economy operates with the speed and effectiveness it does is due to the fact that banks are extremely adept in recording the cash and keeping huge records of all transactions. When you purchase something using debit cards the bank you use communicates with the bank of whomever you're purchasing from. The bank subtracts digitally the amount from your account and the bank then adds money to the customer's account. If the records don't meet, that could cause an enormous issue.

If you purchased a burger at $5 and the bank took $5 off your account, however the restaurant's bank added $100 into their accounts, you'll find that the bank added $95 to the cash account with the click of the button. Banks are able to stay in business because they're extremely adept at keeping these records in order. If a bank couldn't manage this effectively would go out of business, and its employees might be facing the possibility of prison time.

The cashless economy isn't something new. It's ancient. Most money, during the majority of the history of mankind was not in the form of cash. It was mostly stored in ledgers, much like in banks. Ledgers are a listing of sales and purchases. The oldest ledger known is just a couple of thousand years old and was written on clay (Dockrill in 2016,).

If Brad purchased some 2 x 4s for $80 from Steve, Steve would write an entry in the form of a book that they had were both in agreement that Brad would be willing to pay $100 for the 2 x 4s. Both parties would sign the note to prove that Steve was not swindling an offer. Brad could walk away with 2 4s and the cash was never transferred. The signatures provide proof of the transaction in the event of a dispute later about it. This is exactly what bank cards do However, earlier, ledgers were a mix of individuals' personal ledgers. If everyone's financial statements are in good standing there is no need to look for anyone who can pay the debt. The system is able to function with no cash payments for quite a lengthy time, provided that the participants trading in this manner trust each with enough trust that they don't attempt to cheat and not settle.

Modern banking operates in the same way , however, faster, electronically, and with less trust requirement between two parties. What crypto can do is maintain an accurate record of transactions, without the requirement of more than two banks, or an processor for payments. Crypto can help us avoid three middlemen during transactions. This is a hugely important technology.

Cryptocurrencies such as Ethereum and Bitcoin function by creating an extremely long, decentralized ledger that is referred to as blockchain. When a transaction is completed there is a new entry made to the blockchain. Every couple of minutes, a new "block" that contains transactions will be added. Each block is a reference to the prior block, which makes them into an "chain." This is all the blockchain has to offer. A collection of ledger entries, exactly as a book of ledgers that we could have read just a few hundred years ago.

Similar to the ancient ledgers, the blockchain does not exist on just one computer. It's available on many computers. Users who provide their computer power to manage the blockchain functions are known as "miners." Mining creates new crypto for miners in exchange by using computers and electricity to perform this task.

The block created cannot be modified. It's write-only. It's forever. Every time a block gets placed on the blockchain mining computers are able to communicate with one another and need to come to an agreement. Computers compare their blockchain records with those of others and verify each other's work. If a new block added to the chain isn't compatible with any other computer, it is rejected. Each computer, working in isolation, must maintain their integrity.

The only way to hack or modify the chain is to fool every computer that is that is evaluating the work simultaneously by hacking each block following the first hack and be able to accomplish this feat so quickly that it can accomplish this feat without the first block is added. This is only feasible in the realm of science-fiction. As of now nobody has an iota of the computing power needed to hack blockchains.

This was an overwhelming amount of information to dump at you at once We'll highlight the most important points to ensure that it gets absorbed into your mind. You must be able to comprehend this prior to moving ahead.

* Crypto is not money. The cryptocurrency is an asset similar to precious metals.

* Crypto is the blockchain, which is an extremely complex and sophisticated ledger. It's basically a record of transactions that show who did whom what and the dates.

* Crypto is present on many computers around the world which work together to keep the system running as well as free from counterfeiting.

The reason why Crypto is valuable

The better question is "Why is cash so valuable?" In the end, cash is simply paper. The value of cash is in its role as a currency as well as the fact that anyone can accept the cash of a solvent mint and, most importantly, to conduct business in a foreign country where you are required to pay by using their money. Governments will only take their own currency as tax purposes.

Crypto is highly valuable due to similar reasons, however it's not backed by the confidence and trust that any other government. We have discussed before what makes value. Certain items with certain characteristics at specific times will always be of value. Crypto has some inherent qualities that make it superior to other types of traditional fiat currency printed by the state or gold.

The reason is that cryptocurrency is totally exposed. There is no room for hiding in the world of blockchain. The information on blockchain is available to the public. Anyone is able to view it. Everything is running in ledgers' calculations nobody is hiding the money, nobody is able to steal, and no one is able to transfer money without being seen.

Since the owner of cryptocurrency-wallets is private, this is a great option for privacy-conscious individuals who do not want to be the target of corporations or governments who like to monitor the way you spend your money. This could be due to legitimate, legal motives. It could be used for illicit actions like sales of weapons or drugs. Any type of market transaction whether it's white, black, or grey, is private as long as the wallet's owner's ID is secure. There is no need for credit checks or a photo ID to buy or sell cryptocurrency. The usual restrictions banks must notify the government whenever they notice suspicious signs aren't in place in this case.

People who are sceptical and uneasy about the power of government and monetary policy frequently discuss the possibility that crypto will be inflationary. When you use any government-backed currency, the nation's money policy is managed by competent, but they are also prone to error. They may be successful but, as we've observed throughout the past, if they fail it could be catastrophic. The government is able to increase or decrease its money supply by adjusting the interest rates of its central bank. When the government increases its quantity of money available it is likely to cause a similar increase in prices because more money is used to purchase less products. This isn't an issue for a reliable and financially sound cryptocurrency. A cryptocurrency such as Ethereum has a highly predictable inflationary plan.

"What is it about NFTs?" you may be thinking. "What is it that Bitcoin and Ethereum have to relate to NFTs?""

I'm glad you asked because we're only now getting to this.

Digital assets such as Bitcoin and Ethereum have their individual blockchains. They are two distinct things. The majority of NFTs are on the Ethereum blockchain, also known as another "alt-coin" chain created with Ethereum. One of the things that distinguishes Ethereum unique is the fact it is able to store any digital data in its blockchain. This includes music, videos documents, images or any other data that could be saved on computers. Bitcoin isn't able to accomplish this.

These digital objects, such as music and images, are what are known as NFTs. Blockchain is the thing that is what makes NFTs the way they function, and what is unique about them.

Ethereum as well as Smart Contracts

Bitcoin is currently the most popular cryptocurrency in the world, with Ethereum next in line at number 2.

One of the things that distinguishes Ethereum unique is the fact that it has something it calls smart contracts. Smart contracts are similar to a legal contract however, it's written in computer code , and is managed by computers with no need for judges or lawyers. Smart contracts are automatically executing agreement. Every cryptocurrency asset can have an associated smart contract it. The consequences for this type of technology can be huge and we'll explore the subject further on. The most important thing to know at this point is that the rights to property and contracts can be added permanently into the digital asset. This is why NFTs are more than expensive artwork digitally linked to an address on the internet and the reason why Ethereum is essential to this particular story.

Ethereum is a far advanced tech than Bitcoin. Ethereum provides power and maintenance for virtual spaces such as The Sandbox as well as DeFi Space. The Sandbox is an innovative experiment to build an entire virtual world built on a blockchain that is, users who join and build the space earn their own crypto, known as SAND. The rewards are also earned by making and distributing NFTs. DeFi is a short form for "decentralized finance" which is a reference to this brand new blockchain technology, as well as the platforms that operate on it.

Ethereum can also be used to operate NFT marketplaces and blockchain domains. The top 100 most popular cryptocurrency the majority are based using Ethereum's token standards ERC-20. A majority of the "alt-coin" chains utilize the ERC-721 standard of Ethereum for NFTs. "Standard" refers to that the code is interoperable with the code. This is an abundance of confusing words which can be explained by an analogy. There's a standard electricity outlet found in America that is a three-hole wall socket. It is used for the majority of household items. Any electrical item you purchase will fit into the wall socket. It doesn't matter what it's. It could be a lamp or a television, computer, or even a toaster. They all function perfectly using the standard outlet. If everyone uses the same standard for outlets that everyone can design products that work with it because they're interoperable. Every company does not have different plugs to use a different outlet. But the same plugs aren't compatible with all locations in Europe. In the US and Europe utilize different standards that aren't interoperable. The token standard follows the exact concept. The various cryptocurrency assets are based with the exact same Blockchain as long as they adhere to the same standards. ERC-20 is the standard that is fungible. ERC-721 is the non-fungible standard.

The interoperability of Ethereum's assets mean that you can build things by connecting them in intriguing ways. This brings the subject of smart contracts. That's exactly what is the whole point of it. Whatever computers can accomplish, a contract could accomplish. The hottest smart contract comes with an integrated method of paying royalty. Inseparable to the NFT is a code that runs each when the currency is sold. an NFT that has this contract is able to pay out an amount to the creator. This is a way to deposit funds into the artist's cryptocurrency account from now on until the end of time. The most well-known example of this was carried out by one of the first NFT user, Imogen Heap.

The smart contracts form part of NFT. They are not able to be modified or removed. These royalties are only the beginning of what's possible. This means that there is no requirement to refer disputes to the courts of law. A computer runs the program, and it occurs. There aren't notaries, no expensive lawyers to present their case in front of judges, and there's no case law or an interpretation by law of this code. There are no negotiations with record labels, or complicated, public disputes. The contracts are just what they are.

Many athletes who play sports have sad endings after retirement. They often lose money while they're young and don't plan for the future. They don't have money saved or use their money prudently, like young people tend to do. NFTs can be life-saving for those who are like this. Remaining occupants from their work days can assist them in retirement by way of smart contracts.

Ethereum isn't without its flaws, but developers are working on ways of addressing the issues. As of now,

Ethereum is the only true option in the field of NFTs.

Chapter 6: Are Crypto Currencies Safe?

One of the most crucial things to keep in mind concerning cryptocurrency tokens is that they are simply frauds. Because cryptocurrency tokens are simple to make and resell, scammers need to make a token, set up a fancy website and then pay for some ads through social media. Pay for a handful of news sites to highlight their cryptocurrency and then they could become wealthy from novices who aren't familiar with crypto. Naturally the next question that your crypto-curious friends will likely to ask is an old-fashioned one: Are cryptocurrencies secure after all. I've heard of criminals and scammers employ the cryptocurrencies, and I've been researching these hacks. This is the typical answer to these kinds of comments and questions. The safety of a cryptocurrency or not is dependent on the situation first. Different cryptocurrencies were created in the same way. Some cryptocurrencies are designed to be able to speed up transactions over security. Typically the results can manifest rather quickly.

It's good news for us that it is not uncommon to find hackers seeking to break into crypto networks in order to manipulate to create new currency or tokens out of air and sell them at an impressive profit. It may sound frightening however it's no like the way corporations and banks every day. When hackers do succeed in causing damage to a company, it usually enhances its cyber security. This is also true for cryptocurrency which means that the majority of digital currencies that have been around for a long time are thoroughly battle-tested because they are always targeted by criminals. If you're still doubtful take a look at this as I have mentioned earlier. Certain cryptocurrency networks consist of computers scattered across the world which are continuously double-checking transaction history and balances of accounts. If you wanted to compromise the cryptocurrency network, you'd be required to hack over half of computers that are connected to the network in order to do it. It isn't possible to do this when you are dealing with an exchange such as Bitcoin that is comprised of millions of computers distributed across the world. But, some cryptocurrency networks have less computers processing transactions, making them more vulnerable to hacks. Similar rules apply to the centralized cryptocurrency service like exchanges for cryptocurrency, where the majority of cyber-attacks have occurred. They are much more easy and more lucrative than a single cryptocurrency wallet, which is incredibly safe. This is the reason you must always keep your cryptocurrency inside your bank account. When you can and only store it on exchanges when trading or cashing out . When speaking of security, there is nothing better than an actual wallet.

In fact, when it comes to criminal activity they almost always trade bitcoin in exchange for a security-focused cryptocurrency such as monero. If they can as bitcoin, like most cryptos, can be viewed publicly for transactions as well as balances in the wallet. Bitcoin transactions are easy to track by authorities, and even more than conventional currency. It is absurd for criminals to regularly make use of and possess an asset that can be traced. Cryptocurrencies such as monero are private so even the US government can't break the encryption. It's quite impressive when you consider the entire picture. the vast majority of cryptocurrency are not utilized for illegal purposes. There are only a few in the crypto market that thieves employ.

The main danger with cryptocurrency and investing in cryptocurrency is volatile. In the sense that the prices could fluctuate up to 50x the course of a single day. The risk of investing too much in crypto could be very risky particularly if you try your luck using leverage, which makes use of borrowed funds. This is the reason it is best to only invest the amount you're willing to risk and not risk a cent more.

Why are cryptocurrency's prices so unstable?

What's the point of them having any worth? Here's my answer. What is it that gives the money you carry around in bank any value? At one time it was backed by gold, but this was changed, and ever since all currencies issued by states around the world are losing value. The reason for this is that the only thing that holds euros and dollars is the trust we place in the governments who issue these currencies. That trust is eroding over the last many years. And not just that, governments have been making and manipulating currency in order to profit them and the companies that finance them, at the cost of the ordinary person. This has led to record levels of inflation that encourage savings over spending and leads to excessive consumption and causes environmental disasters.

The value of cryptocurrency is due to their capabilities. Their value fluctuates depending on the cryptocurrency we're discussing. Bitcoin is worth its weight because the BTC coin has a similar economic profile to gold. There is a limit on supply and only a tiny portion of BTC is produced every day. This amount is divided into two halves each four-year period. If demand for bitcoin remains the same throughout time, this will cause a significant increase in bitcoin's value each four-year period. The demand for bitcoin has grown in the past few years as we have realized how fragile regular currencies can be. The current epidemic has heightened the recognition of this fact as economics dictates that something is in an insufficient supply. But there is a demand is continuing to grow, causing prices to rise. Many investors consider bitcoin as a safe way to keep their capital out from the financial market, which includes myself.

The most important point to keep in mind is that all other cryptos are closely linked to bitcoin. Their prices are dependent on the way that BTC does. Even although that's the case, certain cryptocurrencies like Ethereum are extremely valuable due to the value they offer. The Ethereum network is used to make those crypto tokens that I mentioned earlier. It is possible to develop decentralized websites and applications that are not censored and stop any transactions that involve creating and transporting tokens. The use of these applications requires ether in order to cover gas expenses. This means that the demand for eth increases when the Ethereum network grows in popularity as well as Ethereum has seen significant use. Visa has begun testing payments using the Ethereum network by using the USDT token that I previously mentioned. It is the European central bank has even issued an obligation using Ethereum. Ethereum blockchain.

The reason for price of BTC, ETH, and any other cryptocurrency fluctuates daily is because nobody really knows the value of these technologies. Prices of stocks and gold, and even conventional currency fluctuate daily because of the same reason however, cryptocurrencies are more volatile due to the fact that they are completely new. Cryptocurrency networks enable you to save, lend and even borrow without a financial score, credit card or even bank. They allow you to do business directly others without intermediaries making a profit. That means service giants such as Uber and tech giants such as Facebook might be deemed obsolete. They allow groups to pool their resources in a single account and then vote on what they should spend them on which eventually eliminates governments need and corrupt politicians. One could claim that crypto is the equivalent of an technological innovation that could threaten the power of the current power structures. The potential for this can make the average investor in crypto extremely nervous that even the tiniest chance of a government clampdown on crypto could result in an economic crash. Even the most outrageous rumor could cause a huge market resurgence in the long period. But, it is clear that crypto is growing , and the growth will not end anytime in the near future. In the present you've probably somewhat convinced your friends that crypto is a legitimate business.

What cryptocurrencies should I purchase?

Before I answer this question, it is important to keep in mind that I do not serve as your financial advisor or an investment consultant. In the event that your cryptocurrency investment fails, you will be the one to blame. The cryptocurrencies you choose to invest in will be based on your risk tolerance and timeline. Regarding timeframes the cryptocurrency market appears to follow a 4-year cycle. It is now in the bull-market phase that is when prices rise gradually. the cryptocurrency bull market may end this fall, and possibly up to early 2022. The chance of selling your cryptos at the best prices is little to zero. But, the majority of cryptos have seen the majority of their gains in this bull market. A 3-5% rate of return is feasible. It's even more likely when you decide to wait until the next bull market in crypto.

Fun fact is that purchasing and holding crypto will earn approximately the same amount of money when you are actively trading cryptocurrency, which I don't recommend to do unless you intend to take it on as a full-time career. Risk tolerance may be a bit snarky given that cryptocurrencies are risky investments However, there are various levels of risk within the cryptocurrency market. In reality, the greater risk you're willing to take, the better rewards you can expect to earn. One of the most efficient ways to gauge risk and reward is to consider the market capitalization of cryptocurrencies. This is a crucial measure to look at since the value in dollars of cryptocurrency can be deceiving.

The market cap of a cryptocurrency is calculated using the current value of the token or coin multiplied by its circulating supply. Dogecoin is so high because it is circulating an amount of 130 billion after which, when multiplying that number by the price of 30 cents for dogecoin that gives you an additional 40 billion dollars market cap. You might believe that dogecoin provides the perfect chance to make money quickly however, to reach one dollar will require more than 80 billion dollars in active investment. This isn't all that likely to occur as a rule of the thumb. The lower that the market capitalization, the higher the potential cryptocurrency will grow, regardless of its value in dollars It requires less money to boost the value of its currency.

For a more extreme example, yearn Finance's wi-fi token has a higher value than bitcoin. But its market cap is only 20 times that of dogecoin's. This means it will require less capital to increase the price of wi-fi, excluding dogecoin and a few other cryptocurrencies. Most of the cryptocurrencies on the list of top 10. Based on market capitalization, they can be considered as investments with low risk. Cryptocurrencies such as Bitcoin, Ethereum, and Cardano will likely to be present for a while. They'll likely increase by a factor of three or more in value before the current market turns down. The other 90 cryptos in the top 100 might have gains of 3 to 5x, however the lower you get on to the bottom of the pile, the more risky the investment is due to the fact that it takes less capital to lower their prices. I would recommend staying clear of any cryptocurrency that's not within the top 200 in terms of market cap since the majority of the top projects have already emerged from the bushes and any move further would be a gamble.

Chapter 7: Eyes Of The Eagle

NFT Industries to Watch Closely

Fads may be a thing of the past However, they will become more prominent.

There's a lot more that I could add This is my attempt to understand the meaning of the long-running NFT industry. The following categories have grown and grow.

Games:

The use of NFTs in games is an obvious choice. There are billions of dollars spent on the skins, upgrades and power-ups and more. Why should they not pay for it when they receive an #NFT you can exchange? Axie Infinity is on track to surpass half a billion dollars in revenue. That's $AXS valued at $4 billion. The first of many.

Art:

Art has been collected over long periods of time. It's just a way to increase the digital dimension. When we begin exploring VR/AR/AI, I'm not sure what the artists will create. One of the most profitable NFT industries, generating between $10 and $50 millionplus volume over the past 9 months.

Collectibles:

There's not much that needs to be said about this. There's a sense of belonging and joy when you own or collect something you want. This includes punk, rare Pepe games, rock or other game items.

Sports:

We witnessed MLB play an online fantasy league collectible sports game back in the beginning. This is a rarity also NBA Top Shot is taking this idea to the next level. Owning cards/figurines/moments of your fav players and using them in games.

Metaverse/Virtual Land:

This is a broad idea. Many believe that we're all moving toward a virtual life across many, interconnected virtual spaces. Take our identity, our assets and community with us. Virtual living could be an option that we can own by NFTs.

Finance:

Your NFTs could be utilized as collateral, rented and fractionalized so that many people have access to them or used to fund an insurance plan, utilized to stake them and obtain fees discounts and so on. Utilizing NFTs in financial protocols is becoming more commonplace and will continue to grow widespread.

Identity:

Making use of NFTs to create Avatars using social media applications or in virtual worlds, is already an option. When they are integrated into web3 applications, they are able to be identified and allow access to other features. E.g. Discord channels that are not locked by NFTs.

Fashion:

Clothing, wearables, or whatever you like However, if we're to live in digital worlds then we'll have to make our avatars look good. Right? Bitcoin, Decentraland is one of the early tests. Brands that are luxury are emerging the market as this sector grows.

Access:

Access virtual clubs in Decentraland, Access to time with Gary Vee, Access to Mark Cuban, access to airdrops, NFTs work exceptionally well with access to people/projects/spaces. We've seen a few experiments however it is one of the largest services offered by the technology.

I'm not able to help but think I've missed a few Feel free to add your own. The above timeline is an attempt to illustrate the place where these industries began.

It's possible that I'm wrong but the bottom line is that they've been in development for some time before the hype of this year.

Chapter 8: How To Create A Nft Free Of Cost

The NFTs (Non-fungible tokens) are difficult to get off the internet in recent times. In the event that you're a crafter or performer, or perhaps someone else creative, you might have researched ways to create an NFT. If so then, you'll probably have discovered that it could cost you at least $100 in "gas charges" an essential cost to manage and approve transactions that are made on Ethereum. Ethereum blockchain.

This is just to create the NFT and we're not, at all considering selling it. It isn't possible to avoid fees associated with selling NFTs (for instance, paying the cost of your transactions to commercial centers) However, there's an alternative to get out of these charges during the printing process. We'll discuss how you can create an NFT absolutely free of chargeand why you should think about it, regardless of whether you'll never sell one.

The solution I would recommend is known as S!ng. It currently is available only for iOS but the company plans to release the macOS application very soon, and then eventually Android but there's no specific timeframe for the final option. You'll be able to access the web form if you've sought assistance with your iOS application, because the web version isn't available as an alternative.

Whatever the name, S!ng permits you to create virtually any type of NFT that includes the ability to capture images, audio or recordings through the application, and an uploader for documents to be uploaded to different kinds of content that can be turned into an NFT. This is crucial since there is no way to alter features, so unless you're sharing something in the idea stage it is necessary to use the technique of record transfer.

The benefit of S!ng, and the reason I'm using it in this particular model is that you do not be knowledgeable about digital currency or NFTs to make use of it. simply install it on the App Store and create your own record and then you're good to go go. It even creates the Ethereum money-saving account, which can store your data. This is usually a distinct approach to most administrations which requires the making of another record.

When you've logged in to the application and have entered your email address, you will be asked to sign up for assistance. After that you'll choose the name you want to use on S!ng and identify what kind of manufacturer you're from a list of 10 possibilities.

You are now ready to start an initial NFT and it's easier.

Press the round button on the bottom of your screen.

Select the symbol that corresponds to the item you want to create or transfer (File or photo or video).

Take or transfer the substance.

Alternate the name of the NFT in the event that you want to.

Notes, colleagues or related documents by pressing the in addition button to secure.

Tap Submit.

The application is now able to generate your NFT. This took just a few seconds to create the images that I used for my test documents, but the amount of time required will depend on the size of the document you're moving and the speed of your company. S!ng definitely tested with up to 150GB documents, but there is no specific vertical limit for the size of records.

Congratulations! You've earned an NFT! The software will allow you to efficiently browse, save or even share your NFTs to others.

It is essential to know that NFTs that are printed using S!ng can be facilitated by AWS and IPFS The final option is a document arrangement on blockchain in the form of. NFTs operate using the Ethereum blockchain, which uses the ERC-721 standard. This is a fanciful way of saying that regardless of whether or not S!ng disintegrates, due to the fact of the Ethereum organisation, your data remains impeccable (aside of the AWS storage; you'll be unable to access the stockpiling).

What is the best way to make money selling your NFT using S!ng?

The section of the story that's not included in S!ng is an establishment that sells your NFTs. The company is planning to launch one by the time the month is over but in all likelihood that it does open this will become a closed commercial center that is made up of a curated group of musicians. The content will not be limited to music only, however visual specialists will be working with artists to create the content they will release for their NFT releases.

The aid will eventually extend beyond music, but just like the title music is the center of S!ng. The Chief Product Director will be Raine Maida, the lead singer for the group Our Lady Peace. He views the program as an opportunity for crafters to connect in a more direct way with their fans and provide an original product for them without the interference of an outsider.

For those who don't have the status of a celebrity S!ng is trying to provide a combination together with the largest accessible NFT commercial hubs, meaning that anyone who has the application could certainly sell their performances. This assistance is expected to be offered very soon, in line with S!ng, and we'll provide instructions as soon as it is available.

Why should you make an NFT in the unlikely event that you do not intend selling it?

Whatever the reason, regardless of whether you intend to sell an NFT there are many reasons to use S!ng. It was initially conceived as a way for innovative minds to collaborate with a clear and undisputed trace of who invented the idea and when. The blockchain is the best solution to this because it lets you publish content with a safe and clear timestamp which is automatically updated by the blockchain providing evidence of the initial invention.

The pioneers Jim Harmon and Geoff Osler recognized the expansive implications of this, and created Maida with their assistance it was adopting its new music center. The ability to make use of the basic innovation and allow clients to use the next NFTs was essentially an added benefit.

The need to secure the validity of licensed innovations (IP) will be more crucial than at any time in recent history, as we can easily share content via the internet. Maida was referring to TikTok for instance. The stage's two-part harmony lets users play off the other's content while still recognizing the other. It creates an enthralling environment for interaction between the creatives, but it also carries risks with regard to the IP that is introduced into the world of trades.

No matter if it's an alliance between craftsmen, innovators scholars, artists, software engineers or any other maker that are able to exchange and transfer information while keeping an unmistakable guardianship chain of the IP is extremely valuable and S!ng is determined to make it as simple as can be desired.

The choice of making an NFT for absolutely nothing

There are various options to create an NFT at no cost, however they're not as simple to use. One of them is OpenSea which is probably the largest commercial NFT center. If you don't have an iOS gadget , and are keen in selling and making NFTsthen this could be the best option.

OpenSea is fairly straightforward in terms of record creation and provides a lot more comprehensive assistance for different types of content. However you must first create another Ethereum wallet and connect it is linked to the OpenSea account. It assists in walking you through this process beginning, however it's not as consistent like it is with S!ng.

It is also notable that it doesn't have a program for creating NFTs. Although this isn't a problem for large projects that are scheduled to be bought, it does not provide with some of the other advantages for creatives S!ng gives, for instance, the capability to make an NFT The second motive is that it's a surprise.

Chapter 9: Common Mistakes Made By Nft That You Should Beware Of

Before diving head-first to the terrain of NFTs There are a few most common mistakes you should steer clear of. While the development and sale of NFTs isn't running for a long time however, it is evident that some individuals make the same mistakes time and repeatedly.

These mistakes could result in a disaster for your progress on this NFT world. There is a good chance that you will make some minor mistakes as you're starting out and that's fine. So long as you take the lessons learned from these mistakes, they are okay. The most important thing to be doing is be aware of these major mistakes that could be the difference between success and failure.

1. Thinking too short-term

Certain NFTs have gone for millions of dollars over the past year. However, that doesn't mean you can make NFTs and invest into them and earn a significant amount of money in the first attempt. If you attempt to make excessively fast money by using NFTs and you fail, it's likely that you'll fall short and drop the whole concept.

It is obvious it is true that the NFT journey is an exciting experience. However, this doesn't mean you will be a millionaire the end of next week, however. If you approach NFTs with an "get rich quickly" approach, then you are very likely to not succeed.

The best method to be successful in the field of NFTs is to create value. Also, you must possess a lot of patience since you may not be able to sell your NFTs immediately. Keep up with your marketing and marketing efforts, and make the effort to create partnerships and collaborations that will benefit you in the near future. If you're committed to playing the NFT strategy, you must be committed to it in the long time.

2. Are you not doing enough to promote your NFTs?

It's not enough to start your NFTs, then list their details on OpenSea and expect the funds to start coming into. There are millions of NFTs who are on OpenSea and the majority are having difficulty finding buyers.

Don't be fooled by your "build the foundation and then they'll follow" idea. This isn't likely to occur. It is essential to develop your own marketing plan, and follow it. Find out who your audience is, and then determine the places they go to hang out.

Make use of social media platforms to boost the power of your NFT promotions. Utilize Discord Forums, Clubhouse and Reddit to your advantage, too. Make every effort to make sure that people know about your NFTs and the skills you possess.

There are some who might be luck with NFTs. They could put them up on OpenSea and sell them in a short time and then have people beg to buy more. These kinds of situations are extremely uncommon. It is impossible to count on this type of luck, so ensure you create a marketing plan and implement it.

3. Selecting the wrong marketplace for your NFTs

This is another common error which we hear about time and time again. NFT creators don't have the time to conduct the necessary study and choose OpenSea since it's the largest platform. Sure, OpenSea has a large number of users (nearly 40 million per month and increasing) however, this doesn't mean that it is the most suitable platform for NFTs.

There are many things you should know about the NFT marketplace prior to using it. The most important is knowing if your intended customers use this marketplace. It is important to determine if the NFTs you wish to build are a great to fit with the spirit of the market.

There are a lot of new NFT marketplaces popping up all every day, it is important be sure that the one you're thinking of making use of is secure. The amount of people who participate within the marketplace is vital however, more important is the degree to which the community is friendly and responsive.

Unfortunately, there are fraudulent NFT websites in operation. They will simply take money from you for payment of Ethereum for instance, and you are not selling anything. To stay away from these fraudulent NFT websites, you can use this Dapp Radar website to check for authenticity.

4. Cheap NFTs to do

The more you are able to put into your NFT venture, the more you can invest in it. Many people fall into the trap of believing about the world of NFTs is free as they are able to run everything for a low cost. While some platforms don't charge fees for listing, the majority of the top-quality ones do, so you have to consider this in the NFT budget.

We've told you numerous times in this article about how it is the Ethereum blockchain system is far the most popular of NFTs. If you are interested in using the Ethereum network, then you're likely to be required to pay for gas.

It is important to put cash into your NFT marketing, too. If you do not have a massive fan base on Facebook, you'll have to utilize advertisements on social media to promote your NFTs. This is an affordable method to get results quickly.

Although it is possible that listing and gas costs will fall when NFTs become more popular, it cannot be assured and you shouldn't be sure of this occurring. If fees do decrease in cost, you can use the money you saved to invest in additional marketing. You must be prepared to take this NFT process seriously. be ready to invest your money into it to give it the best chances of success.

5. Uncertain of the process NFTs function

There's a reason we have included an entire chapter on how NFTs function earlier inside this article. We've seen many people make costly mistakes due to the fact that they were not aware of the fundamentals of blockchain technology and crypto.

It is crucial to are aware of the way NFTs operate and how blockchain works. If you're required to read the chapter again take the time to do so. We've tried all we can to ensure that the text is as simple to comprehend as we can however there are certain technical aspects of NFTs and blockchain that you must grasp in basic terms at the very least.

Chapter 10: What To Do To Locate High-Quality Nfts

NFTs are selling for many thousands. you may be thinking: what can I do to find one of these incredible NFTs? In this article I'll show you three ways you can locate important NFTs.

It is believed that the NFT below is an drawing of italic Buterin that was auctioned for 141,000 ethereum price and you may be thinking what the reason for paying such a high price for a digital work of art? This brings us to our method number one, which is:

Making an NFT, being an Influencer, or buying NFTs from a person of Influence

The painting that appears above was designed by a person known as 'Trevor Jones'. this artist has gained an image in NFT artwork. Therefore, when they make a painting the public is pretty much purchasing the image.

If you are influential or an online platform, it can be a marketing source. We can see this in the creator of "Rick and Morty" Justin Roiland; as soon the artist creates a work of art, people are aware about it, and they believe in his name.

This is something is evident in the everyday art world. People don't have to pay for the work printed on paper, but they are paying the artist, and that's the way it works. Similar things are happening within the NFT art world , but most of the people that are reading the book people with influence or have an audience, but don't fret I've got you covered and will show you how to overcome this obstacle.

Justin Roiland who has a following decided to start his own NFT art collection. Of course , it will get immediate exposure and is bound to be sold. If you visit Niftygate You'll notice that this is the site where Justin Roiland has decided to showcase his collection.

It's evident that the majority of the pieces are sold out. If we click on "eligible bachelors' which is a part of the artworks there it is clear that there are 100 pieces , but they've almost all sold.

A key aspect of NFTs is they are not fungible tokens meaning they're scarce, and sometimes only one available. The reason for this is that investing in NFTs is different than investing in traditional cryptocurrency. If someone has done all of the research necessary for a cryptocurrency-related project and finds that their research suggests they should purchase, they are able to duplicate their trades, but keep in mind that NFTs are not unlimited, meaning that when there's only five available, they can't conduct all the research before they copy the trade, and then purchase it since they'll need to buy it from its owner.

In this area I'm not telling you what to buy , but I want to show buyers how to purchase, as it is more important to know the best way to purchase. For instance, with this particular Rick and Morty creator, it's now being resold on the market , and we can see "eligible bachelors' who are selling at various price points

If you're at this point you may feel that you're late. However, if you're not an individual with influence, and don't have an online presence, the strategy I'm going give you is to get attention from a person with influence and I'll show you an example. Logan Paul is a person with influence who will publish NFTs and, since you're familiar with Logan Paul or maybe another popular person, and you are following their Twitter and Facebook accounts, you'll be aware earlier than other people that they are going to issue an NFT.

It's not my intention to suggest you buy Logan Paul's NFTs This is just an example. If they do decide to launch the NFT it will be able to purchase it before anyone else however, the danger is that you might purchase an NFT that nobody else is interested in.

You may be able to purchase it at an affordable price, however it might not be possible to sell it again after.

Another way I want to use is:

Gaining traction from Influencers

This strategy can help reduce the risk. For instance, let's suppose that Logan Paul releases NFT and one person buys it for hundred dollars, and the next day, someone purchases it for one hundred and fifty dollars , and immediately an additional person purchases it for 200 dollars. It is evident that it is increasing in popularity, and this could be a great opportunity to buy it if there is a trend where consumers will pay more however if you get in way too soon, you may purchase something that nobody would else wants.

In the above image it is clear how Lindsay Lohan and tiger the rapper are immediately accessible and are currently the one of the top-selling artists on Rarable but keep in mind that we're not the ones who have influence What could we do instead is follow the people who have influence and gain some traction.

You may be the most influential person in the world of crypto art Christie's auction house is planning to offer NFT art by the famous digital artist Beeple. What is Beeple?

Beeple is a guy known as Mike WinkeLmann and he's a father from Wisconsin who drives a bit of shitcorolla.

This is a normal person who has built his own reputation and influence in the world of digital media and it's possible that you make a random artwork on Rarable and perhaps someday, you'll be this person and the work could be sold but the chance is low. It is more likely that you'll be able sell NFT art that is worth buying when you purchase the artwork from someone who has established a name.

It's not like I'm throwing the concept of making your own NFT out the window It's your choice to go ahead and become the next who mania, or the next Michael Von winkelmann.

The second strategy is not dependent on the influencer's reputation however, it does involve;

Reputation of a Platform Reputation of a Platform

If we examine the top-priced NFT that are sold will find that they be sold on these same networks.

The NFT (9 land plots of genesis) in AXIE infinity was sold to 1.5 million dollars. As we can see it on the list above, there was a second version from AXIE infinity that was sold for one of thirty-six thousand dollars. Also, we can see another NFT from cryptopunk, which was sold for seven hundreds of forty-seven thousand dollars, which is known as alien. the image below shows what it appears to be.

Another platform that lets you purchase and sell trading NFTs on trade is OpenSea If you sign up to openSea then you are able to proceed and trade this cryptopunk. The same applies to cryptokitties. OpenSea offers everything you could imagine, but the majority of the products on these platforms don't sell.

What we have learned from the first approach is that you cannot create an NFT on these platforms and hope to sell it at the highest price, however you can follow the process to gain popularity. Let's look at an instance using NBA; NBA top shot is an NFT platform that's not built on ethereum. it's built on flow blockchain developed by dapper labs and allows you to use and purchase and sell NFTs.

It's true that the majority are of the NFTs are extremely expensive right now as we can see LeBron James NFTs going at $200,000. The method we'd employ to gain traction is to take a look at LeBron James's NFT. LeBron James NFT, note that we're a bit late with this particular NFT however I'll demonstrate how you can accomplish this using more recent NFTs that aren't sold priced at the moment.

If we look back in the past of this NFT and let's say that we were at the beginning of the market and we were following the market, we observe that the initial price of sale was $1500.

It was then sold for $1780. was purchased for $1780, and later it was purchased for $2000 . It will be at this point when we'd know this NFT is getting more attention. After a couple of sales, we can observe that people are buying it and it's increasing in popularity. It's approximately $2000 which I would like to join. Of course, some rates might not be suitable for some people, but the fact is that this is what's about NFTs as a type of game that you pay.

There's a myth that says that NFTs are simply jumping into the market and creating an art, and you're rich, but that's not the case. The only way that this method can work is if you're an influential person and have an opportunity to sell your services If you're not one of those people, then you'll need pay for the privilege in order to acquire one of these useful NFTs.

If we want to go to the NBA top shot and take a look at the lower costs of NFTs in the current market

It is evident from the above image that there are NFTs are trading against

$2 $3, $4 and so on. This is the right time to should invest in one of these NFTs and look for signs of gains. Will people purchase the NFT? This is possible on any platform, and every when you click an NFT it will display the past history.

It will also show what other bidders were bidding and reveal what the buyers were willing to pay. If you are in the early hours and pay attention, and see that an NFT was auctioned for $100 and $150 , then $200, $300, and $800, you'll be aware that it is gaining momentum and that is your starting point.

The two first methods heavily depend on reputation or reputation of the individual or the reputation of the platform, however the third option does not depend on reputation as much, and this is:

Space of Domain Names Space of Domain Names

If we visit OpenSea We can find that some domain names that are there have been purchased for a price that is high.

It is interesting to note that all the names are extremely short; amazon. Eve, wallet. East, crypto.eth and what we learned from the prior dot com bubble was that individuals would be willing to shell out a significant amount of money to acquire a valuable domain. Dot coms have been sold for millions dollars

In the case of opensea, the main thing to remember when purchasing the best domain name is to buy something using only one word. However, there are times when you can manage with just two words, as we've observed with carinsurance.com. As you will see, many of the most desirable domain names are extremely short. Three-word domain names are unlikely to be as valuable in the near future.

You'll now be betting on which of these closing domain names will prevail There's dot eth as well as dot crypto. dot zil, which is for zilka, and other domain names available. We've seen with dot com that cars.com is an excellent investment however cars.net isn't, so the bet you're taking in this case is gambling on which among these names is going to win in the next 20 years.

Could the name be Dot Crypto? Could it be dotzillaka? Dot Eth or another however, it doesn't end there. It is still necessary to find an initial name that is small And there's two ways to accomplish this:

We'll use the approach of gaining momentum for those who want to own an extremely lucrative domain with just an exact word, such as jobs.If you do, then you'll need to sell it on the open market and pay a premium it or even begin by scratch.

As you will see from these methods It doesn't give you what to buy , but helps you choose what to purchase and one thing that we've observed across the three strategies is that getting traction might be the best choice. Don't be too early could lead you to purchase something that isn't wanted by anyone however, if you're purchasing something that is getting attention and is gaining traction, it will give you an indication that it is worth the money and that people are interested in it.

Chapter 11: A New Future Of Nfts - Nfts' Growing Potential

The NFT sector is extremely new and is constantly undergoing rapid growth. Because of NFTs being new and being a disruptive force in the realm in digital asset, their future is largely unknown. There is no way to know what is in store for the future of NFTs. The degree of innovation and technological advancement associated with this field is a strong potential candidate for a future-generation technology that is likely to be a defining influence within our daily lives. In contrast the ineffective management of NFTs could cause their demise. This chapter we will try to explore what the future holds for NFTs and how they can grow. The numerous aspects that will contribute in making NFTs will be discussed. NFT scene will be further discussed.

8.1 The NFT market is the next tech bubble

The rise of the NFT market has been driven by the astronomical investor interest, which brought an abundance of new players into the industry. It is believed that the vast large portion of transactions in the NFT market are conducted between people who want to profit from this latest trend. The rapid growth in the NFT market led to fears of a bubble developing in the market. A bubble in financial terms is an economic cycle in which the value of assets increases rapidly. If the bubble bursts, the assets usually fall in value.

To determine whether it is appropriate to use the term "bubble" as a description of the market at present NFT market, it is necessary to first look at how interest in NFTs is likely to alter in time. While the majority of those that are involved in

NFTs are investment firms, some buy NFTs to collect them. For instance, there is a collector of digital art known as Cao Yin, who saw the worth of NFTs at as early as 2017when he bought his first NFT for between $2,000 and $1,000. In just five years the NFT increased to approximately $1 million. Despite the potential for massive profits from trading the NFT to buyers who are willing, Cao Yin chose not to let it go and has decided to keep it in his collection of digital works. He is part of the growing number of collectors who have demonstrated a great willingness to invest in digital artifacts.

Although these collectors see a clear benefits in investing in the digital world, Cao Yin goes on to claim that "there's the possibility of a bubble. There are many bubbles , and the bubbles are very large. However, the gems and masterpieces are undervalued". This lets us draw connections between the current NFT market as well as the $370 billion global collectors market and the possibility for stunning digital artifacts to become worth the same value as the $8 million Qing Dynasty Vase or the $31 million Codex composed by Leonardo da Vinci. Since we can track the background of every NFT through the blockchain, the historic works of the future might be made in the near future. There's a great deal of digital work currently being created and although most of them will fall into the shadows but there will be some which will become desirable and sought-after.

8.2 Relationship to Cryptocurrencies

The use of cryptocurrency and blockchain technology is rapid. NFTs will likely benefit from the growth of cryptocurrency as they are generally interconnected. This is due to the fact that NFTs are traded exclusively through cryptocurrencies on NFT marketplaces. In keeping their value in the respective currencies in constant supply they are expected to increase as the price of these currencies increase. As more money is put into investing in market for cryptocurrency, we could anticipate a part of the capital to make its way in NFTs. NFT market. It is therefore possible for NFTs to expand in the same way as that of the crypto market. This seems to be very positive for the NFT market.

8.3 Digitalizing Existing Assets

There's a different intriguing use for NFTs which is that they can be used to digitize existing assets. Smart contracts' capabilities for every NFT will allow people to manage their assets on a higher levels. The application of NFTs could allow existing red tape from legislation to be streamlined to create the most efficient outcomes for all those who are involved in the management of assets.

In the beginning, assets like property and shares could be tokenized. The foundation has been set to ensure that the change can be completed smoothly. With NFTs the representation of assets is as efficient as it was in the past. But, NFTs provide a wider range of capabilities that could encourage the transfer of assets to NFTs.

8.3.1 The Shareholder's Voting Rights

Traditional assets like company shares can provide an abundance of benefits for investors. In the first place, it eliminates the need for long-winded documents of ownership. Voting shares tokenized can allow shareholders to participate more efficiently when making decisions. Traditional taking votes on decisions requires the presence of all the major shareholders, in order that they are able to reach a consensus on the decisions that the business must take in the future. This could result in cost of travel and travel that are not beneficial to everyone involved. If the share certificates are tokenized the ownership of these shares could be verified via a remote connection, which will permit the voting process to take place without the need to bring together all shareholders. This will help accelerate the process of making decisions because there won't be the need to delay business decisions until an upcoming shareholder's meeting.

8.3.2 Trusts

Trust funds can today be established with specific conditions of when the funds will be distributed to beneficiaries. For instance an trust fund may be created by an individual who wishes to distribute $200,000 to any family member after they successfully complete their college. Smart contracts are able to be created to carry out the wishes that was made by the individual who set up the trust fund. For instance, the contract can allow to redeem $200,000 following the receipt of an NFT connected to the confirmation that the member of your family has achieved completion. The creators of smart contracts are assured that their choices are carried out in the manner they were designed even after their death. This is an issue since contracts are frequently made to be interpreted by the courts, which can lead to lengthy litigation. In a nutshell, choosing to utilize intelligent contracts or NFTs to make financial and legal agreements would provide more value when compared with conventional legal systems because there will be a greater chance that the stipulations will be fulfilled more precisely.

8.3.3 Insurance Policies

Like conventional venture capital markets it's believed that NFTs will dramatically enhance the field of insurance. It's not uncommon for insurance companies to require many forms of documentation as well as a myriad of complex steps to handle the insurance claim. Even if the claim is legitimate and the money from the company could be delayed until it reaches you. In the insurance business it is essential to be more efficient to solve these issues and all of this is made possible through NFTs. Additionally, they can be used to develop plans for the development of new forms of medical insurance. These includes insurance policies designed and implemented upon the availability of evidence. If you are ill and are hospitalized, you may be presented With an NFT issued by the health facility which shows that you have been injured in a specific way , and thus are qualified for a particular insurance claim. You are then able to redeem that issued NFT at your own expense to get the payout amount. This is not just saving the time needed to process the paperwork, but help policyholders get their insurance claims faster.

8.4 Exponential Growth

NFTs are likely to adopt the form of an exponential model. This is due to positive feedback loops which increases the benefits of NFTs. At the time that NFTs were first introduced in the early days, there was a dire need for trust to be created around the legitimacy and idea of NFTs before any interest was generated for NFTs. It is the reverse too. There must be enough interest in NFT so that a firm consensus about the idea and validity of NFTs is able to be established. This means that once enough interest is generated then a positive feedback loop could be developed, and the rise in interest may be a catalyst for more widespread acceptance of ownership by NFTs which, in turn, helps to generate more interest in this NFT space. This chain reaction indicates the possibility that the NFT space expanding exponentially.

The best part about NFTs is the underlying principles for their use have already been established. NFT as a viable representation of ownership for digital assets has received broad support and has resulted in a high level of interest to NFT. The trend is likely to continue to grow and self-reinforcing, and will eventually result in a massive integration of NFTs in our modern financial systems and societies. This will be likely to result in an unimaginable amount of capital flowing into NFT markets.

8.5 The Blockchain as well as NFTs are a Superb Data Management Solution

In many ways the blockchain is an ideal option for managing data as contrasted to traditional methods for storing data. First of all, the data stored on blockchains can never be changed and are not changed. Anyone who wants to have access to information stored in the blockchain will be confident that the information is true as there is no way to prevent altering the data. Blockchain's decentralization capabilities can also make it highly secure as there isn't any single security breach. Traditional data centres, hackers might be able take, erase or alter data should they be able to break through the security mechanisms that are in place for the facilities. However the decentralized network that is the basis of blockchain technology means that even if hackers are able to access a single or even multiple nodes that there will be thousands of nodes scattered around the globe. The advantages of blockchain could provide it with an advantage and could be a major reason for its adoption by companies that need the management of data.

The implications of the use of blockchain technology for the storage of data by companies could be a reality within the next few years. On a company level, businesses can expect to manage many hundreds, or even millions of different digital files each day. All of them can be connected to specific NFTs, which will allow them to distinguish between different files and ensure they are accessible. What this might have for NFT market is that, as companies accelerate the adoption of NFT to mainstream use the acceptance and consensus around NFTs as a substitute for digital files will increase in strength. As the world progresses to this consensus of how NFTs should be defined, NFTs will gradually increase their value due to being linked to digital assets and files.

One of the biggest negatives to blockchain technology however the fact that a huge amount of energy is used in order to run the system, and this can be extremely harmful to the environment and damaging to the environment. This is why environmentalists have voiced their concerns and have criticized the growth use of technology like blockchain. This is a valid concern as the unsustainable nature of blockchain technology could end up being its downfall when environmental issues are emphasized over technological proficiency. The large amount of electricity consumed is due to the Proof-of-Work mechanism that drives the majority of the blockchain of many cryptocurrencies. However, Ethereum 2.0 delivers an efficient solution to this issue by switching to the Proof-of-Stake method, which is more eco-friendly since it doesn't require the same amount of electricity to run mining processes. The stakeholder can rest assured that environmental concerns will be addressed, and these challenges will be eliminated. As the shift to PoS is completed it is possible for environmental issues to no longer threaten the survival of Ethereum and NFTs.

8.6 After a smart Money

One of the fundamental rules of investing is to follow the path of the smart money. Smart money is the money held by experts who have more experience and likely to be better at recognizing changing trends. In general, the move of smart money to industries and assets is typically and is followed by them doing extremely good in terms of creating yields for investors. For NFTs it is apparent that a substantial part of smart money has found its way into the many initiatives and startups looking to focus on NFTs.

Checks of huge size have been made by venture capitalists in support of startups operating in the NFT scene. Dapper Labs, a blockchain company that has made substantial contributions to the growth of NFTs, has had a valuation of $2 billion by 2021, after receiving the sum of $250 million from hedge funds like Coatue. These investments suggest a an increasing demand for NFT market from institutional investors, which means that we could witness a rising amount of capital from institutions devoted to NFTs. As more capital is poured in NFTs in general and the NFT space in particular, we could have a larger amount of cash flowing into NFT transactions which is generally an indication of positive investment. Startups that are getting more financially supported will likely also dedicate significant resources to the development of NFT capabilities to their maximum potential. Overall the investment possibilities in the realm of NFTs are great and investors are advised to make the effort to learn about the market before investing in NFTs.

Chapter 12: Benefits Of Nfts

With all the hype over NFTs It's worth asking whether there are any benefits of making use of NFTs in comparison to other blockchain-based assets. There are several advantages when you hold NFTs over various kinds of investments. Here are the most significant advantages and advantages of NFTs:

OWNERSHIP

It's no surprise that the main benefit of NFTs is that they have an identifiable and specific owner. Therefore, the NFT owner is completely in control over their assets, unlike others of the crypto-assets. This is since the NFT is unique and can't be duplicated or spent twice. There are no issues in this kind of "stealing" of the valuable item in this scenario. One of the benefits of non-fungibility is the fact that it is not soluble within water. They are also not divisible and have a further benefit. The person who is the owner of a non-financial transactions (NFT) is not able to "divide" their assets into smaller pieces. In the case of an example for instance, if you own an image, you are the sole owner of that artwork. There's not a single inch of it that could be traded or sold. They are also inseparable since they are digital files or record, which makes them unbreakable. It is impossible for a technical reason to physically divide one NFT into two identical parts or in any other way. It is possible to make copies of the NFT in digital format and trade or sell the duplicate as an alternative to the original asset provided that there is access to the original item. Due to the non-fungibility and ownership of NFTs, the owners of them have total control over their assistance and the only person who can use them could claim ownership due to their request. Therefore, when NFTs are employed in apps or games, developers as well as users can be assured that their information is secure. Example: If you've purchased a rare item through the course of a contest or program that you have won, you can be sure that it's safe and no one could claim ownership of the item in question. Since your asset is not fungible, there is no possibility of losing your investment in it.

TRANSFERABILITY

Additionally, one benefit of NFTs is that they are easy to transfer between people. This is possible due to the blockchain's ability to make it easy to track transfers of tokens that are not fungible. In addition, because they can be identified with an unique ID number NFTs are much more transferable than most

other assets that are based on blockchain. The owner of the asset can use an ID number to exchange or sell the item swiftly and easily without providing any additional details. The players of games and apps which use NFTs can gain from this because it will make it simpler for them selling or trading their possessions. Utilizing a blockchain-based auction system that is integrated into the game the game's creator could allow players to quickly trade or sell their precious items in exchange for other items. This can be accomplished using the simple identification of transactions instead of providing much more information about the item including its place in the game, or the degree of rarity as is required now. Consider the possibility of a digital art gallery that allows people to sell or barter their digital artworks quickly and efficiently. Blockchain-based systems could be utilized to track the ownership of a digital art and allows buyers to trade or sell their possessions quickly and efficiently with a unique ID associated with their items.

AUTHENTICITY

The credibility of NFTs is another significant benefit. The reason for this is that the blockchain allows you to show the authenticity of an asset. It is possible to be certain that the products you are using is genuine and not fake in the case, for instance, when you're playing a video game or using an application that makes use of NFTs. A blockchain explorer, such as Etherscan.io or an electronic signature or fingerprint of an asset that is used in the game or application could be used to determine this.

So, developers will be able to quickly and clearly prove that their products are authentic and haven't been copied or altered in any way. The users will feel more secure when they trade, purchase or sell NFTs within games and applications due to this. Additionally, the legitimacy of NFTs allows developers to track the amount of times an item was used in their applications.

Therefore, it is easy to find out the number of times the item has been used and the frequency at which it was sold or bought. It is possible to do this by taking a look at the amount of transactions through the blockchain with an explorer for blockchain. Developers can quickly identify how well-known their assets are , and the value they could be able to offer in the marketplace.

SECURITY

One of the main benefits of NFTs is that they are safe. Since each NFT is identified by an ID number that is unique It is not possible for anyone to "copy" or "clone" one of these devices. That means that you are able to be sure that your valuables are safe and won't be taken or duplicated by a third-party at any time in the future.

In games and applications that use uncommon items as a reward or achievement method for the players involved, this can be particularly relevant when it comes to using NFTs. It is possible to be confident that the rewards you offer to players who achieve certain goals in a game that uses NFTs are not counterfeit because NFTs are not able to be replicated or manipulated in any way.

CUSTOMIZATION

The possibility of customizing NFTs is another significant benefit. This is due to the fact that NFTs can be changed easily by users and developers to represent any thing they want.. Imagine a game designer creates an entirely new virtual sword for their game , which players can utilize to battle against their foes. This is referred to as the virtual sword.

Then, they can modify the look of the sword by choosing from a set of elements that define the characteristics of the sword including its length, size of weight, its weight, and the amount of points for attack as well as other factors.

In the beginning, gamers will be able to collect different swords, each having unique features and characteristics that could give them an advantage over their opponents when playing the game.

It is also possible for developers to create "generic" asset types that can be altered by users thanks to changes in NFTs. Take the following example where an application developer creates an avatar of a sword without any particular features or metrics associated with it. In addition, they can allow users to customize their weapon with additional attributes and stats through an editor in the game or an integrated mechanism within the application the program itself.

Customized swords created by players with unique attributes and stats that are based on their individual tastes and preferences can be used in the game or within the within the application. It is possible for developers to create individual assets that represent anything they like due to the ability to modify NFTs. This can be done by simply altering the characteristics and the statistics of an asset, in addition to the image of the asset the item itself.

PERMISSIONLESS

NFTs don't require authorization is a major benefit. This is due to the fact that NFTs can be used by anyone at any time without the need for approval of anyone. Developers will be able to quickly and easily create new tokens and assets for their games and apps without requiring permission from anyone else.

This allows developers to have a level of flexibility not possible in other blockchain-based assets, such as currencies or tokens. Additionally, they don't need to worry about limitations on the kind of assistance they could develop or the variety of assets that they can include in their applications and video games.

In addition, the permissionless nature of NFTs makes it easy for users to sell or trade their assets on the open market without having to obtain approval from anyone else. This allows users to sell or trade their goods easily and quickly. It also provides an environment that is secure and safe that allows them to trade or sell their items without having to worry about the privacy of their personal data.

It is also beneficial for developers because the non-permissionless nature of NFTs permits them to more easily incorporate their own assets into applications or games because of this. This is because they're not restricted by restrictions regarding the type of investments they can make or the quantity of assets that they can provide.

Chapter 13: The Downsides Of The Nfts And Crypto Currency

Non-profit organizations (NFTs) can open opportunities for musicians, there are disadvantages and risks that you must take note of.

Copyright and ownership are key concepts to grasp.

Art theft is becoming more common in NFTs. Recent reports have emerged months of artists discovering their work sold on the internet and being advertised as toys that are not functional (NFTs) without their permission or knowledge.

This is due to the foundation that NFTs operate on was developed a few years ago , and it hasn't been modified to reflect the way of how internet users are able to exchange and sell assets that are not decentralized like art.

An earlier version of NFTs was packaged in an 2017 "game" known as CryptoKittties and is based upon the idea that quantum computing could be used. A small number of virtual cat (sold in the form of NFTs) were available for purchase and players were able to breed them with other players of the game. But, since the NFTs were created in the hands of game's developers in the time they were only available within that specific game's environment.

Because the creators owned the sole rights to animals that were able to be bought or sold, the user was not able to upload a copy of a cat for sale or use to benefit themselves. Since the creators had total control over who was able to develop new cats and also had total control over the number of cats that were available on the market at any given time. The market for cat breeds would not expand due to this.

However, when it concerns the art industry the creators of NFTs (in this case digital artists) are not in control on how or where their work is displayed and sold. The an artist from Wellington Pepper Raccoon argues, this was a problem prior to the advent of NFTs into the picture and the vision that NFTs want to give artists isn't as appears to appear to be on the surface.

"I don't believe that NFTs can be effective in resolving all the problems claims they're successful in resolving. It's all about selling hope." As we've said before, the benefit for NFTs lies in the fact that their document of work is a guarantee that the original item you purchased comes with a unique token with it, meaning that the owner of it is aware that they own an "original." The problem is that someone could take the JPG and put it up on another marketplace, with another token associated with it, then later sell it at a profits. "There there isn't an "original.'"

Who has the power to "mint" an NFT and who doesn't? The answer is simple that the artist should have all the control over the production and distribution of his work (i.e. the number of "original" versions are offered for sale) and also the places where their work is made available to purchase. However, due to the symbiosis on the web, turning the idea to use is a challenge.

If you think about the financial challenges that artists have faced over the last year, it's not surprising that the thought of selling their work online appealing. It's not difficult to understand the reasons why some artists have turned to selling their work in non-financial items (NFTs) to survive when you add the recent, hyped, world of cryptocurrency. In the end artists must conduct an investigation into platforms that promote original works and then choose the items that are sold to avoid their work from being stolen off by other artists.

"There are many other options for selling digital artworkthat are available]," Raccoon explains. "Art Grab is an impressive website that was launched recently and accepts money in fiat as a payment method. You can license images and then it will be deleted from the web, and you'll be proprietor of that image. It's just normal money being employed.

Based on the way it's arranged is an appreciation of the artist, not simply putting up one million dollars worth of merchandise. As I consider it I think it's extremely curated and I think that this has much to do with the way in which value is defined. Instead of saying, "here's an exchange with eight million anonymous tokens you can purchase' it states, "These are artists that we are convinced of, artists who are doing innovative activities and challenging the boundaries" instead of "here's an anonymous market for tokens in which you can purchase."

Environment

Similar to the way it is true that the NFT mechanism is outdated The Ethereum blockchain, the platform on which NFTs are constructed is also outdated and unable to keep pace with the magnitude and volume of global, rapid adoption.

Ether Ether (cryptocurrency) that is located within Ethereum's Ethereum blockchain, along with its counterpart Bitcoin can be "mined" (or "produced") by normal people who use computers to solve mathematical issues. The people who mine the coins receive them to thank them for their work to mine the cryptocurrency. The more coins increase the more incentive for other people to get involved in mining. It's basically a symbiotic relation that if I scratch me, then I'll do the same to my and vice versa.

The problem is that the energy needed in the mining of Bitcoin or Ethereum is huge. Take this for instance the power required to create the new Bitcoin produces greater carbon dioxide emission than the entire nation of Aotearoa to put it in perspective. According to estimations, Bitcoin is on pace to exceed the total energy consumption of London. London.

"A single artwork that is sold in a non-financial transaction consumes about two weeks of energy from the home in a single transaction" says Raccoon. "

A growing number of NFT markets are considering moving from an "proof of work" system (in which computers have to solve certain mathematical equations to create the new currency) to an "proof of stake" system (in which coins are produced through placing wagers on an outcome) (in which players have to prove ownership of their coins in order to create fresh coins). This is why provable stake systems (also called system of proof of stake) tend to become increasingly popular.

Users could effectively show that they are the owner of a portion of the land (or blockchain) and thus increase the value of the asset, and also allows for the creation of new blocks that will create greater value.

Could this sweeping change impact positively the warming effects of blockchain technology? Maybe just for a short time. But the carbon emissions that are associated with Ethereum or Bitcoin mining are rising rapidly which requires a substantial amount of research and development to solve the issue fully. This kind of innovation is costly in terms of time and money in the short being, the economic benefits outweigh the environmental impacts that will be long-term for those who take part.

The environmental impacts of mining ethereum has prompted some artists to end their NFT efforts completely until more eco-friendly methods can be employed.

Obstacles that prevent entry as well as the flow of money

A lot of influential and wealthy individuals across the globe invest in Ethereum and, consequently they have a keen desire to see the cryptocurrency grow. According to Raccoon these investors who make the huge checks that made headlines during the last few years. According to the writer "the bigger art acquisitions that you can see happening such as the Beeple's purchase for $69 million artwork and the $69 million purchase of Beeple's artwork, were made by a person who is vested in the growth of cryptocurrency."

Due to the 'pyramid' structure that is inherent in its NFT method, it can be extremely difficult for artists who are new to climb to the top of the ladder. A lot of artists have difficulty to promote their work due to the fact that they do not have a following or even a name. In the words of Raccoon, "the individuals at the highest in the hierarchy that have already established themselves, the artists who have released NFTs and have a huge following , are the ones who are making the most money." "A majority of people believe in the possibility of making thousands and even thousands of dollars but, actually, it's another concentrated traditional art market" according to the author in the publication.

What can artists do?

Raccoon is not afraid to voice her opinions.

"Wait and watch," she advises, she adds that "the notion of imagining worth must be viewed with caution." If you're sold the idea that your work is worth something that's not real - or has virtual value online and that you can earn money by your work. It is crucial to think about the place where your money is going. That's why I believe that putting it off is the most efficient method of action."

It is important to note that the NFT market is in its early stages, and, as with other emerging markets it is facing certain issues with its teeth and is causing several serious concerns regarding its future. Are we going to see it be a disaster? Or will it grow into an easier to control platform which will reduce the risk of copyright infringement as well as existing power systems that currently prevail in the market? Are there new, more efficient platforms emerge to address the energy-intensive technology elements in the near future?

It will take time to answer these questions. While there has been some discussion about the insanity and ethical aspects of non-profit organisations (NFTs) but the most important thing is that artists ought to be able earn an income through their work without worrying about creating an unsustainable pyramid scheme, the destruction of the ecological balance of the Earth, or the opinions by their colleagues.

Perhaps it's true that this NFT market has created an important discussion about how artists can earn income from the selling of their work in a world which is becoming more centralized.

As per Raccoon, investing in a "get rich quick" strategy that harms the environment is morally wrong and damaging. "Artists must be honest and with a purpose," he adds. The impact of selling non-traditional works artwork (NFTs) can be significant because there's a substantial part of the art market that is so completely off by this, that you'll lose some of your viewers, and artists must decide if the risk is truly worth it."

When you consider the negative reaction to artists who use unconventional methods of earning an income, it's crucial to keep in mind that these artists aren't the cause of the problem.

Despite being aware that it can be simple to criticize or slam other artists for taking part in NFTs, says Raccoon, "we need to be a community at final analysis. artists should encourage sustainable ways of earning an income." "[The artists] aren't the ones to blame for the issue; instead, it's the method by which Ethereum is constructed and also those who profit from Ethereum which are are the ones causing the issue."

There are Real Downsides of Cryptocurrency

A significant amount of the time was devoted to in praising the benefits that blockchain tech and cryptocurrency throughout this article. On the other hand the negatives of cryptocurrency have been a reason for some (such as the well-known investment guru Warrant Buffet) to label them as the next "bubble" in the world of finance. Recognizing and understanding the negatives and barriers that could hinder wide-scale acceptance of these technology is essential in this regard. Particularly,

Drawback #1 Scalability

The challenges associated with scaling that cryptocurrencies offer are the most significant of problems. Although the amount of digital currencies as well as their use is growing rapidly however, they are far behind the volume of transactions that giant of payments VISA is able to conduct every day. Additionally the speed of transactions is another important metric with which cryptocurrency will not be able to compete on an equal basis with businesses like VISA as well as Mastercard till the system supporting these technologies is massively increased. This is a complicated process and is difficult to accomplish in a seamless process. But, other researchers have proposed a variety options to solve the issue of scalability, such as lightning networks and sharding and staking as well being other alternatives worth considering.

Drawback #2: Cybersecurity concerns

Since they are a digital technology they are susceptible to cyber-security breaches and could end up in the hands of cybercriminals. There is already evidence of this with several first coin offering (ICOs) getting hacked, and investors losing millions of dollars just in the time of summer (one of these hacks alone led to the loss of $473 million in the hands of investors). Of course, reducing the risk requires continuous upkeep of security infrastructures but we're already seeing numerous players deal with it directly and taking enhanced security measures that are superior to those used in conventional banks.

Price volatility and the absence in intrinsic worth are three remaining negatives.

In the cryptocurrency market price volatility and its connection to the absence in intrinsic worth, has become an important issue. It is one of the points that Buffet made explicit mention of in the past few weeks when he described the cryptocurrency ecosystem as being in an economic bubble. It's a legitimate concern however, it could be addressed by clearly linking bitcoin's value to tangible and intangible items (as we've seen emerging players with diamonds and the energy derivatives). Furthermore, the confidence of consumers will increase due to the an increase in adoption, which will aid in reducing volatility.

Drawback 2: Cybersecurity issues

In his remarks, buffet also addressed this problem, saying "It does not make sense." There's no regulation to be followed for this. This is out of control and uncontrollable. The central banks or even one like the United States

Federal Reserve, or any other central bank has authority over it. I have no confidence in this endeavor. "I believe that it will fall to the ground."

If we can develop the technology to the point of perfection and eliminate all of the problems mentioned previously. If that happens however, there is a more risk involved in making investments in the technology until it's approved and monitored through the government of the United States.

The most popular of the concerns about technology is operational in the sense that they are logistical in. An example of this is changing procedures, which is essential as technology develops can take a lengthy time to complete and result in a slowdown in the normal business process.

The key conclusion is as follows:

With all the possible challenges to widespread adoption, it's only normal for experienced professionals to be skeptical of investors like Warren Buffet would want to remain safe with regard to the technology. However, we're sure that cryptocurrency (as as well in the field of blockchain) will be in use for quite a while. They provide numerous of the benefits that people are looking for in a cryptocurrency today such as decentralization, transparency and the ability to be flexible are only some of the benefits they bring. The discussion should be extended to encompass everything blockchain technology has the potential to provide in a variety of industries strengthens this claim further.

Chapter 14: Selling And Making Of Nft

If you're interested in trying making the NFT by using your digital art This is a step-by-step tutorial.

Many artists are now pondering what they can do to promote and build an NFT. They still spark debate and fury due to the high price at which certain NFT works are sold. It's natural to be interested in knowing if NFTs are a way to make money from your work If that's the situation.

This book will assist you to know how to build or sell NFT If this is the situation.

But, they aren't common circumstances and, even if are able to duplicate their success, you'll notice that the bulk of the funds isn't going to you. Companies that facilitate transactions and platforms that create and maintain

NFTs are charged NFT artists various fees prior to and following every sale. They could even take you out of cash based on how much your work is selling for.

There are currently several online websites that let you make or sell NFTs. Auction sites that are popular for buying as well as selling NFTs include OpenSea, Rarible, SuperRare, Nifty Gateway, Foundation, VIV3, BakerySwap, Axie Marketplace, and NFT ShowRooom. Payment choices are MetaMask, Torus, Portis, WalletConnec, Coinbase, MyEtherWallet and Fortmatic.

Purchase cryptocurrency Ethereum cryptocurrency. Ether can be used on the vast majority of platforms.

In the beginning, you'll need pay a platform "mint" (or create) your item. The majority of platforms want to pay the cost with ether, a cryptocurrency that is used by the open source blockchain platform Ethereum that was the first platform where NFTs were launched.

Keep in mind that the price of the ether (abbreviated in ETH) changes dramatically, just as bitcoin and other cryptocurrency. From just under $1,000 in 2021 to nearly 4800 dollars in 2021. numerous peaks and valleys in between it is known to change in the hundreds in just a matter of minutes.

To buy Ethereum it is necessary to set up an "digital digital wallet" and then connect it to the NFT platform you prefer. There are many digital wallet providers to pick from, but we'll be using MetaMask that is available as a browser-based extension and mobile application to accomplish this. If you'd prefer to use another provider, or you're already comfortable with the concept of digital wallets, and you have your existing one then skip to step 4.

Making an electronic wallet

To make an MetaMask electronic wallet visit the website and click"Download" in the bottom right corner "Download" button that is located in the upper right-hand corner. Since we're using a desktop PC so we download the browser extension but there's an app for mobile devices as well.

When you open your first wallet, it will be instructed to create a new wallet and a seed phrase. It's not necessary to think about what is a "seed phrase" is (it's simply a collection of words that will save blockchain information). If you're a yes then it's just an issue of confirming the terms and conditions, establishing an account password, and then performing a few security checks to ensure your account is up and up and running.

Add money to your account

After you've made the MetaMask account (or another digital wallet) then you'll have to pay it off using Ethereum. It's easy: simply click the Buy button and choose Wyre as the payment method. Then you'll be taken to a website where you can purchase Ethereum with Apple Pay or a debit card. You are free to go ahead even if there's no need to spend money at the moment; all you need to do is wait a few minutes longer.

The connection of your bank account to the NFT platform

The procedure for creating an electronic wallet is the identical across all platforms. Once you've got some Ethereum in your digital wallet to spend, you can choose the NFT platform you like and begin making your NFT. We'll use Rarable to illustrate however there are many various NFT platforms to investigate.

Rarable is one of the many online marketplaces that sell digital collectibles.

Rarable is available via Rarable.com. In the upper right corner of the page, there is a button which reads "Connect Wallet. Click here to link your wallet to MetaMask. A pop-up window will open asking you join your account with Rarable. Choose

"Yes" Then "Connect" and agree to the terms of service prior to verifying your age.

Uploading your file

While GIFs can be used to create NFTs, we suggest making the file using an image editor like Photoshop or Paint.NET because these software programs give the complete control of sizing and the sharpness. To accomplish this you must take these steps to follow: Launch the program you prefer and then create a new picture of dimensions 256x128 with black and white tones (if you are using Paint.NET Make sure Advanced Mode is on). Copy your GIF into the new image, then reduce it to make it fit in the entire image.

You're ready to create your NFT immediately. Click the blue button 'Create' located in the upper-right corner. After that, you have the option to choose to either create a singular idea or offer the exact item repeatedly. In this instance, choose "Single.' In this step you will need to send the file you would like to convert to an NFT. Rarible supports PNG, GIF, WEBP MP4 and MP3 files that are up to 30MB in size.

Upload your file and then you'll be able to see it on the right side, you'll be able to preview the NFT post.

The process of setting up an auction

Pick the auction settings you want to use that you want to use for the auction.

In the following section on the application, you'll be required to decide how you'd like to market you NFT artwork.

Three options are. There are three options available "Fixed price" option lets you determine a price and then sell it to someone right away (similar similar to "Buy this item today on eBay"). "Unlimited Auction" is another option "Unlimited auction" option permits other bidders who bid to make an offer.

Then, "Timed Auction" is an auction that is only available for a specific duration of duration. This is the one we'll select for our instance. The most difficult aspect begins with establishing an acceptable price. Don't set it too low and you'll be losing the money you make on each sale because of the high price.

We'll set the price at 1 ETH , and offer buyers seven days to offer. After that, you are able to purchase it immediately however, before you purchase you have the option to "Unlock when you have purchased". This allows you to supply the buyer you are buying from with a high-quality, full version of your work, as well as other documents via a hidden web page and download links.

The option that is labelled "Choose collection" is one of the most confusing options. It's a technical issue regarding how blockchain works. The default setting is "Rarible" So we would suggest that you leave it as it is.

Include your NFT Description

You can now add a title and a description to the ad for your item. To improve your likelihood of selling an

NFT it is important to consider thinking about the idea.

The questionnaire will require you to select the portion of royalties you'd prefer to receive in the event that your work is sold in the near future. It's all about determining a new balance. Higher percentages can bring you more profit in the long run however, they hinder other individuals from selling your work, as they stand lower chances of making an income for themselves. Additionally, the file properties can be included as an additional field. In this case, you're almost finished.

Make payment for the fee

Simply click "Create the item" to begin the process of liaising. You'll be asked to connect your account if there isn't enough money in it. If there's not enough money in your account Don't fret it's not necessary to start from scratch. Click the wallet icon located in the upper right-hand part of your screen. You can add money directly inside Rarable.

Be aware of this prior to doing this. The cost of listing may appear quite low. However, it's just the beginning of the expenses you will encounter. To generate your NFT You will initially need to pay an additional fee of $42.99 before proceeding further in our case.

In addition to the costs to purchase and sell NFT There is an amount of commission when someone purchases your asset, in addition to transfer fees to complete the transaction.

From our point of view we could not find anything adequately clarified on the Rarable website when we attempted to use it.

CPSIA information can be obtained
at www.ICGtesting.com
Printed in the USA
BVHW042317150223
658635BV00010B/186